THE
POWER
OF BEING
DEBT
FREE

How eliminating the national debt could radically improve your standard of living.

THE
POWER

How eliminating the national debt could radically improve your standard of living.

OF BEING
DEBT
FREE

ROBERT H. SCHULLER
AND
PAUL DAVID DUNN

THOMAS NELSON PUBLISHERS
Nashville • Camden • New York

126414

Second Printing

Published in Nashville, Tennessee, by Thomas Nelson, Inc. and distributed in Canada by Lawson Falle, Ltd., Cambridge, Ontario.

Printed in the United States of America.

Library of Congress Cataloging in Publication Data

Schuller, Robert Harold.
  The power of being debt free.

  1. Debts, Public—United States.   I. Dunn, Paul
David.   II. Title.
HJ8119.S45   1985   336.3′4′0973   84-29453
ISBN 0-8407-5461-2

★ ────────────────────────────

Dedicated to our unborn children and grandchildren with the hope that someday they will be able to secure a thirty-year, fixed-rate mortgage on their home at 7 percent.

CONTENTS

★ ─────────────────────

ACKNOWLEDGMENTS

We would like to thank Dr. Milton Friedman, Dr. Gary Shilling, Dr. Arthur Laffer, John Templeton, John Crean, J. Peter Grace, and Dr. Martin Feldstein for their valuable contributions to this book. We also extend our gratitude to Lawrence M. Stone, editorial vice-president at Thomas Nelson Publishers, for his guidance and expertise in this project. And special thanks to Jeanne Dunn for her love, encouragement, and countless hours of tirelessly organizing, typing, and editing this manuscript.

INTRODUCTION

★ ────────────────────────────

Robert H. Schuller

It began as a pleasant dinner with friends. Senator Robert Dole, his wife, Elizabeth, and I, together with my traveling companion and producer Michael Nason, were at the Jockey Club in Washington, D.C. The time? Mid-year 1984. Bob told us of the economic challenges the Congress was facing. How could the federal budget deficit be kept under control? What could be done to curtail the rapidly accelerating federal debt. A balanced budget? That was out of the question. Reduce the federal debt? That thought was in nobody's mind. After all, first things first! How do we get control of a runaway deficit economic condition?

"Wouldn't it be wonderful," I said to the Republican senator from Kansas, "if in looking at the federal budget we didn't have that huge chunk called *interest on the federal debt*." I continued, "If there was some way we could irradicate that federal debt responsibly, sensibly, we would be able to have a balanced budget and still maintain a strong and compassionate social consciousness in delivering care to the genuinely poor and needy people in our society. We could also maintain a strong defense against amoral international aggressors."

As soon as I brought up the subject, all of us intuitively sensed that we had listened to the airing of an idea that was utterly impossible!

At the same time, my mind was thinking about the thirtieth anniversary of my Southern California ministry. For thirty years I have been the pastor of one church. And I have learned one important lesson in these thirty years: any great idea that—if it could be pulled off—would prove beneficial to the human family had better be taken seriously no matter how preposterous it sounds! The greatest ideas that come from God are always humanly impossible!

We spent the entire dinner talking, fantasizing, laughing, and alternately becoming serious on the far-out possibility of eliminating the "interest on the federal debt" item from the federal budget.

What is my background for considering such fantasizing legitimate? In 1955, with only a few hundred dollars and no property, I was assigned to begin a new church on the West Coast under the auspices of the oldest Protestant denomination with a continuous ministry in the United States: The Reformed Church in America which started in 1628. For more than twenty years I've enjoyed enormous success. My secret? "Borrow as much as you can, as fast as you can, to go as far as you can!" was the advice I gave myself and others. We borrowed our way into success!

That was possible when interest rates were 6 percent—extended over thirty years! That was possible when we were experiencing a quarter of a century of growth in real estate values!

And yet through all those years it was my job to balance the budget. And it was always tough to look at that chunk of our budget called *interest on the corporate debt.*

In 1955 our budget was $12,500. I watched that budget grow until on the eve of our thirtieth anniversary year, sitting at dinner with Senator Dole and his wife, Elizabeth, I now had the responsibility of balancing a budget of $40 million. "Bob," I said to the senator, "it's a wonderful feeling today, not to have an interest on the debt item in my ministry's $40 million budget! After thirty years we're out of debt! The entire debt has been paid off! What a tremendous surge of inner power and freedom that gives me! I can't begin to describe it! I dream of the day when the power and the freedom that I feel by being debt free can also be enjoyed by the federal government! When that happens the government's power and resulting privileges will filter down to every citizen in our land!"

I left the dinner and found myself inexorably driven to respond to an enormous inner challenge: to apply the principles of possibility thinking that have brought success to my life and to my church to the enormous fiscal challenge that faces our country.

People who know me understand that I work with people who are smarter than I am when I tackle a tough job. I look for bright and intelligent people. Therefore, I asked Paul David Dunn to join me in studying the problems of the federal debt and to co-author this book. Paul's brilliant academic record and successful business acumen impressed me profoundly. Together, we met with economists, businessmen, corporate leaders, senators and representatives, and tried to ask the right questions and address them to the right people. The result of our study is submitted with our prayer that a grass roots mood might build in momentum to create a national commitment to stop what is a disastrous financial trend. The economic goals of the American society must be turned around until our children and grandchildren can enjoy the power of being debt free.

When you encounter the pronoun "I" in this book, you can assume that it is Robert Schuller speaking. When you encounter the pronoun "we," you can assume it is the joint expression of the co-authors. Our ideas have mutually blended so much that it is frequently difficult, I must admit, to know what words came from which pen. The interfacing has been quite remarkable.

It is often said that the best defense is a strong offense. We propose that the best defense against the mounting federal deficits is a strong offense. If we start with a strong national commitment to give our grandchildren a country that is debt free, the pressure would be before us to minimize waste, maximize productivity, and reduce and eliminate deficits. We submit that it is possible to be a debt-free nation!

Recently I talked with my friend, the attorney general of Minnesota, Hubert Humphrey III. "Does Minnesota have a debt?" I asked. "Oh, no," he answered, "Minnesota doesn't have a debt." California is also a debt-free state. There are even a few nations such as Singapore that are debt free. There are many corporations that are debt free. And any institution that has managed to eliminate its debt is in a most unique position of incredible power today!

The goal of being a debt-free nation is possible! And the power it can release for the future is awesome!

If you are ready to think bigger than you have ever thought before—then read on!

Yours for a powerful America tomorrow!

Robert H. Schuller

INTRODUCTION

Paul David Dunn

The year was 1979. I sat in an eight hun-
dred-year-old coffee shop in the old city of
Jerusalem sipping Turkish coffee and
reading an American newspaper. A small article caught
my eye. "U.S. Budget Deficits Approach $35 Billion."
The amount seemed insignificant as I thought about
the strength of my native country. It didn't have the
turbulent financial or political problems of the small
segment of the world I was then in. The U.S. was, in
my mind, an endless power source and strong-hold. I
tossed the newspaper aside, unconcerned with America's financial status.

But during my time of living in the Middle East, I
saw what debt can do to a country's economy and way
of life. When I first arrived in Israel, the exchange rate
was seven pounds to a dollar. On my most recent visit
in 1984, the exchange was 5,000 pounds to the dollar!
In 1984 inflation was over 400 percent. But Israel is not
alone. Other countries around the world, such as Mexico, Argentina, and Brazil, suffer from the ravages of
excessive debt.

As my years abroad passed quickly, I returned to
the United States and learned that our deficits had

grown to more than $100 billion a year. Forecasts for the future were more frightening, with projections for a $200 billion deficit in 1985, rising to 1.5 trillion in the next fifteen years, and a total debt reaching $13 trillion.

What would the economic condition be of the country my children would be born into. How could America handle such an enormous debt? What could be done? I doubted that anything could be done. But then I remembered the words of William Shakespeare who said, "Our doubts are traitors, and make us lose the good we oft might win by fearing to attempt."

As I talked with Dr. Schuller about our nation's debt, he also encouraged me with his version of Shakespeare's advice: "What great thing would we attempt to do if we knew we could not fail?"

The answer for our nation's economic future seemed obvious to us: pay off the national debt. That would eliminate the major cause of our rising budget deficits.

But how can it be done?

In seeking the answer to this question, we interviewed top economists and government and corporate leaders. As we met with these people, I listened intensely and made volumes of notes to help in the writing of this book. I experienced a continuous excitement as the idea of a debt-free America seemed more and more possible. As we explored the factors leading to the budget deficit crisis, we were able to come up with ten possibility-thinking solutions to take us on our journey towards a debt-free nation.

History is often written by people who believe in a dream so intensely that they are willing to commit themselves totally to the realization of that dream.

This book is written with the hope that it will create an awareness of the financial crisis facing America and will rally people behind the dream of making America stronger than it has ever been before. *The Power of Being Debt Free* is written with the hope that Americans will continue to demonstrate the qualities of freedom and democracy that have made our nation great. Perhaps the greatest challenge facing America today is to put our fiscal house in order—to right the future course of America's financial strength and ultimately its ability to export human freedoms and values worldwide. Every generation of Americans faces new challenges and new opportunities to give positive direction to the future of our nation.

The real wealth of America is not merely in its financial statement, but in the great ideas of its people. The concept of a debt-free country is a powerful idea that can change the course of America forever. We are committed to the realization of that dream.

It is our sincere hope and prayer that you will share in this idea and commit yourself to this dream. Together it is possible. Together we can make it happen!

For our future generations,

Paul David Dunn

1

Stealing from Our Children

The young father bounded silently up the deserted stairway to the third floor of the hospital maternity ward. His tennis shoes squeaked on the top step. He waited breathlessly. Had he been heard? Visiting hours were not until 9:00 A.M. He glanced at his watch. It was only 6:30 A.M., but he had to see his wife and tell her the good news. He opened the door, moved quickly through the hallway, and slipped into his wife's room.

"Honey, I had to see you. You'll never believe what happened! Last night I got a $700 bonus from my boss. I bought a new crib, blankets, and some toys, and I even paid off the rest of the medical bills not covered by insurance. We don't owe anything!" he declared excitedly.

"How wonderful!" the young mother smiled with a sense of relief. Just then the head nurse entered the room with a scolding but forgiving look. She allowed the excited father to stay.

Today was the joyous event the proud parents had long awaited as they prepared to take their newborn son home. The nurse helped the mother into the wheelchair. "It's regulations that you must ride down to the front door," she said as she placed the little bundle of new life wrapped in a blanket in the mother's arms. "Oh, and you'll want to take these home," she added as she handed the father a bundle of cards and a vase of flowers.

As they rode down the elevator the father proudly boasted, "It's all paid for, you know. We don't owe anything."

"Really?" the nurse said with a look of admiration. "This child is privileged indeed to have parents that have planned ahead. I am sure he will have a very bright future."

"Well, we worked hard," the young man replied. "After seven years we were able to save $15,000 for a down payment on our condo, and now that we can handle the payments, we wanted to start our family."

The elevator door opened, and as the nurse said good-by, the father wheeled his wife and new son to the front door. As the mother stood carefully so that she would not disturb the sleeping child, a uniformed official quickened his pace to meet them.

"Congratulations!" he stated enthusiastically as he pushed back the blanket to take a peek at the tiny face. "Welcome to America," he said, speaking directly to the child. "Here is your inheritance from your country." He tucked a small envelope under the child's blanket and turned and walked briskly away.

Puzzled, the father reached down to take the letter. He read the official notice aloud to his wife.

"As a newborn citizen you are entitled to all of the privileges of being a citizen of the United States including 'life, liberty, and the pursuit of happiness,' and great opportunities for personal development. The price you are charged for these privileges is $7,714.[1] You are not required to pay this until you begin earning money, at which time it will be deducted from your paychecks in the form of taxes and inflationary prices. By the time you earn your first paycheck, it is estimated that the $7,714 will compound at the current interest to $120,859."

The father's face tightened with anger as he spoke the final figure. "$120,859! He will never be able to afford a college education. What about a down payment for a home? They can't do that to my child! It's not fair! It's not fair!"

The Real Story

It is not fair, but the sad truth is that all children born in the United States today are met with a burden they cannot begin to shoulder, a burden they did not ask to bear. That burden is the mounting federal debt and the rising federal deficits. When we, the current generations of Americans, spend money that we expect the next generation to pay back or to pay interest on, we are stealing from the disposable income of our children.

It is not fair because we have severely limited our children's number one birthright as Americans—the freedom to grow into healthy and happy individuals in a stable economic society dedicated to the principles of freedom and justice for all. Not only are we stealing income from our children, but we are robbing them of economic freedom; for the debt that we have incurred and are willfully passing on to our children greatly impairs their personal liberty. This is not just unfair; it is irresponsible, unjust, and immoral.

The founders of our country considered freedom to be of utmost importance. Their dream was for a country in which all people could choose their own faith, speak their own views, vote and elect officials to enact laws to ensure each person's rights, and have freedom to achieve financial security through the free enterprise system.

Today all children born in the United States still have these opportunities, but nothing looms more threatening to limit their economic freedom than the growing national debt. Our founding fathers warned us two hundred years ago that there was no threat to our freedom greater than the shattering of our economic base. Thomas Jefferson said it best:

> I place economy among the first and most important
> virtues and public debt as the greatest of dangers to be
> feared. . . . To preserve our independence, we must
> not let our rulers load us with public debt . . . we must
> make our choice between economy and liberty or con-
> fusion and servitude. . . .
>
> If we run into such debts, we must be taxed in our meat
> and drink, in our necessities and comforts, in our labor
> and in our amusements. . . . If we can prevent the gov-
> ernment from wasting the labor of the people, under
> the pretense of caring for them, they will be happy.[2]

Today babies are being born in Alaska, New Hamp-
shire, Michigan, Hawaii, Nevada, Florida, New York, and
California. They are being born throughout our country as
citizens of the United States of America. They are our single greatest national resource. The strength of our nation
tomorrow depends to a large degree on the health and
strength of our next generation. Consider what the future of
America would be if all babies were born with a genetic
defect that would shorten their life span, limit their learning
ability, and affect the development of their potential. If this
condition perpetuated itself through the following generations, what would be the future of our country? The future
depends on the health of the next generation. We can do
something about it. Later on we will give ten possible solutions to the problem of the national debt and also spell out
ten things you can do. But before looking at the solutions,
we must clearly outline the problem.

Currently, our economic health is infected with a dangerous cancer that threatens not only our children's future
but also our future. Nothing can destroy our freedom more
quickly than our federal debt of more than $1.8 trillion and
our yearly deficits of more than $160 billion.

How Serious Is Our Debt Today?

A special committee appointed by President Reagan in 1981 projected that at interest rates of 11 percent, and under current, wasteful government spending policies, the federal debt will grow to $13 trillion by the year 2000, and the deficits will increase to $1.5 trillion annually.[3]

It is important to clarify the distinction between the *deficit* and the *debt*. The *deficit* is the amount in a single year that the federal government spends more than it receives from taxes and other revenues. In fiscal year 1984, for instance, the United States government spent approximately $165 billion more than it took in. The *debt* is the accumulation of all of the deficits of our entire history. Much has been said about balancing the budget which would eliminate the *deficits*. But it will be difficult to do because of our *debt*. In fiscal 1984, 14 percent of the federal budget was allocated just to pay the interest on the debt.[4]

Most people think of the United States national debt as being financed by Americans. But the United States is indebted to foreign nations for more dollars than any other country in the world. The amount of debt owned by foreigners, which the United States Treasury is obligated to pay, is approaching $220 billion. This represents a significant shift in the economic framework of the world.

For decades, the United States was an economic superpower, lending money to countries in need in order to spur their economic growth. Now for the first time in history, the situation has dramatically reversed. The United States continues to lend billions of dollars to foreign countries, but we are dependent upon foreign capital inflow simply to pay the interest on our debt. This saps money out of other countries' economies and makes the United States the largest debtor in the world. We have stolen from our children the legacy of a powerful, economically free country

Federal Debt
(1900–1984)

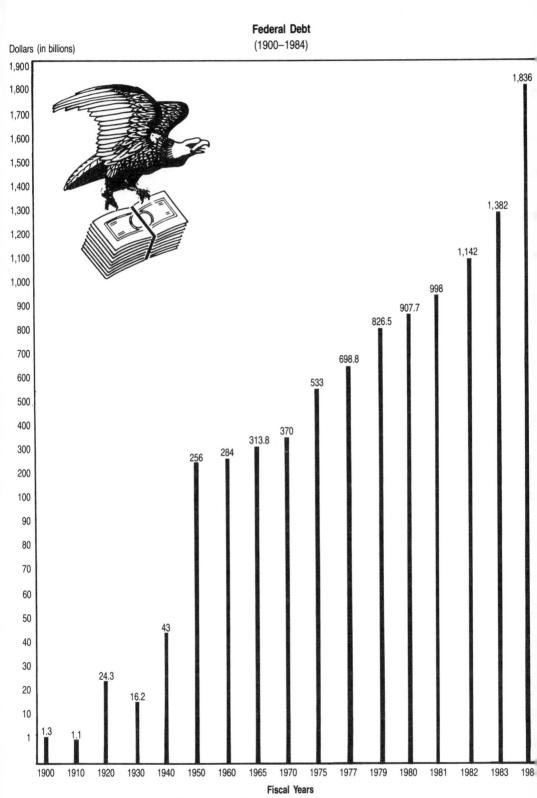

Dollars (in billions)

Fiscal Year	Value
1900	1.3
1910	1.1
1920	24.3
1930	16.2
1940	43
1950	256
1960	284
1965	313.8
1970	370
1975	533
1977	698.8
1979	826.5
1980	907.7
1981	998
1982	1,142
1983	1,382
198	1,836

Fiscal Years

Source: U.S. Treasury Dept, Bureau of Govt. Financial Operatus; Bureau of Census

Federal Debt—Per Capita
(1900–1984)

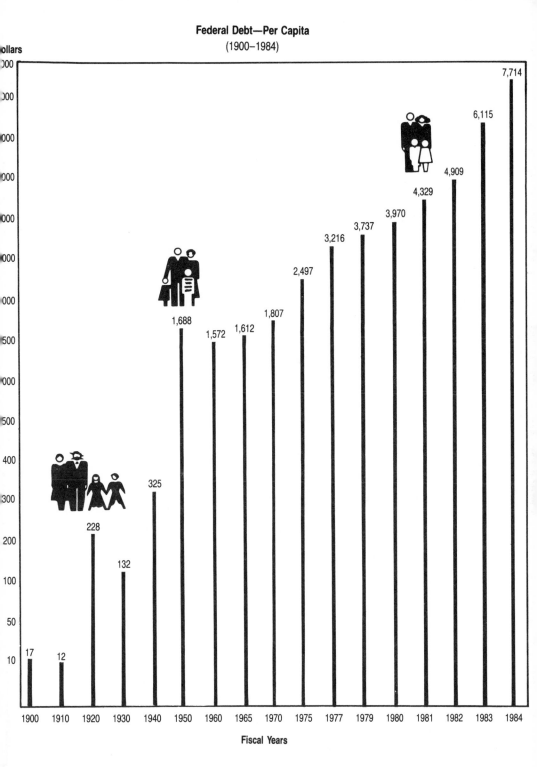

Dollars

Source: U.S. Treasury Dept., Bureau of Govt. Financial Operation; Bureau of Census

Fiscal Years

and given them in its place a country whose economic future may be controlled by others.

Without an inflow of foreign money financing our deficit, interest rates would be substantially higher, possibly three to five percentage points above the current rates. And for every one percentage point increase, an extra $15 billion is added to the federal deficit each year.

Because we need the money, we encourage foreign ownership of our country by promising to pay high rates of return to nations that invest their money to support our rising deficits. We offer high interest rates to attract their money with the hope that future production of our nation will be able to pay them back. To encourage investors, in July of 1984 Congress also passed a law removing a longstanding 30 percent withholding tax on foreign-owned bonds.

In an article in the *Los Angeles Times*, Robert M. Dunn, Jr., professor of international economics at George Washington University, pointed out the severity of this situation: "Advanced nations are supposed to contribute capital to the rest of the world. That is how we help developing countries grow. But the United States has turned this role upside down. We've become a net drain on the scarce capital resources of the world." In the same article, a chief lending officer of one of America's largest banks who specializes in lending money to Third World nations said, "If I were rating the United States as I do other countries, I would put it in the highest of high risk categories."[5]

The rest of our federal deficit is financed by the American public who have invested in their country. The federal government is obliged to pay interest rates ranging from 3 to 18 percent for money invested in the form of bonds, treasury bills, and other financial instruments.

In light of our current astronomical deficit of $165 billion, it's easy to think of deficit spending as a normal gov-

STEALING FROM OUR CHILDREN **27**

ernment practice. But the truth is that out of the 193 budgets our government has had, it has successfully balanced 100 of them. The deficits we have incurred have averaged less than 2 percent of the gross national product (GNP) of goods and services that our nation produces each year.[6] Only five times in history has the deficit exceeded 4 percent of our GNP.[7] The first was at the formation of our republic, and three others were during the Civil War, World War I, and World War II. The fifth time, in 1984, the deficit of 4.8 percent of the GNP was larger than that of any of the previous times of crisis in our nation's history. This percentage is rising despite the fact that in 1984 America was enjoying its strongest economic recovery of postwar history. Perhaps it is this economic recovery that so easily blinds us to the real danger of the encroaching calamity of financial disaster.

In the jungles of Java near Djakarta stands an archaeological wonder. Borobudur is one of the greatest monuments ever erected to Buddha. Built in the ninth century, it covers nearly ten acres, and three miles of bas-relief commemorating historic events in the life of Buddha cover its walls. When it was finished, Borobudur must have appeared to be stronger than the jungle, immune to decay. But as years passed and it was left unattended, the jungle began to encroach upon the edge of the monument. Beautiful green vines growing slowly upon the rock surfaces soon found soft spots and minuscule cracks in which to take their first hold. Surely the vines must have looked attractive and harmless as they curled along the ridge of the monument. But soon, like a giant octopus, the vines overtook it. The quiet, slow-growing jungle overtook the seemingly indestructible temple. Years later, archaeologists cut the jungle back and began to rebuild the broken temple so that it could once again stand as an inspiration to all people.

Our national debt is not unlike the jungle. It keeps growing slowly and quietly with little or no attention given to it. But unless the debt is eliminated, it will eventually engulf our society and strangle our economy. Every man, woman, and child, rich or poor, will pay a higher and higher price for the debt as it continues to grow. Unless the national debt is dealt with in the strongest and most responsible terms, it threatens to engulf our nation.

How Did We Get into This Financial Predicament?

How could the national debt have grown so large? How could it have become so out of control? In the course of our two hundred years, we Americans have faced many crises that justified and necessitated the acquisition of debt. In fact, many times we were forced to borrow funds because our freedom and the economic strength of our nation were at stake.

A child born in 1776, the year our great nation was born, would witness in his lifetime two wars that would pull the country into debt. In the War of 1812 American soldiers went into battle while the new nation borrowed to finance their weaponry. By age eighty-four, that child would watch the young republic split apart in the ghastly Civil War. When the gut-wrenching battles were finished, the United States dug deep into the pockets of its citizens to reconstruct itself so that in 1876 it could celebrate its first centennial birthday.

At slightly more than one hundred years old, America was hit with the depression of the 1890s. We recovered in time only to witness the greatest war the world had yet known—World War I. There were some who felt we should isolate ourselves from the conflict, but under the leadership of Woodrow Wilson, Americans decided to do their part. We wanted to make the world "safe for democracy," as President Wilson phrased it. So again we borrowed and prayed and believed that this was the war to end all wars. When peace was finally at hand, prosperity exploded. Great hopes and expectations allowed us to believe the bubble would never break.

But the bubble burst with a deafening noise during the Great Depression. Voices shouted forth, declaring that capitalism was dead. Masses became enthralled with the revolution that had occurred less than twenty-five years earlier in the Soviet Union, a revolution that promised economic equality to all. Franklin Delano Roosevelt courageously led our country out of this depression. The people voted to borrow the money to create jobs and preserve our free enterprise system. Once again the debt was increased.

Prior to this time in history our debt was tied to the gold standard. But for the first time, the gold standard was abandoned. By an act of Congress in 1934 it was agreed that all printed money would be backed with the collateral of the people's deposits. No longer could we back up our paper currency with gold.

As the debt increased, America faced a second world war. We had been through the War of 1812, the Civil War, and World War I. We couldn't afford another war! But Pearl Harbor gave us no choice. Our survival as a nation was at stake. With Hawaii still smoldering from Japan's surprise air raid, Americans were urged to take their money out of savings accounts and loan it to their country. War bonds were promised to return 3 percent interest on the money that the government borrowed to buy the necessary defensive equipment and finance the military forces that were used to defeat the Axis powers.

With the unconditional surrender of the enemy, we continued to borrow billions of dollars to carry out the Marshall Plan which encouraged us, as a noble and civilized country, not to abandon the defeated nations but to help rebuild them. So we loaned money to European countries and to Japan to launch their new economic and productive recoveries. Where did we get this money to rebuild these other nations? We borrowed money, of course. We increased our federal debt.

World War II was hardly over when we faced an expansionist international Communist threat. The Korean conflict engaged us, and then the Vietnam War drew upon our resources. After a defeat in Asia, our nation was in debt greater than anyone could have envisioned. Today an enormous installation in South Vietnam built with millions of American dollars is used by the Soviet Union as a naval base to harbor its nuclear submarines and other nuclear armaments. When America pulled out of Vietnam, Russia moved in. Not only did we leave with thousands of lost lives, but we pulled out with an enormous debt.

Our $1.836 trillion debt is not only due to wars to preserve our own freedom and that of others, but it is also due to wars on poverty in our own country. We believe that the dignity of the individual is a nonnegotiable human value. Most Americans are willing to share their wealth to keep children and elderly people from starvation, to provide employment opportunities to all who are able to work, and to offer a high quality education to all young Americans.

In the early 1960s John F. Kennedy started the Peace Corps to promote world peace and friendship. Peace Corps volunteers still share their technical knowledge with people in less developed nations. Later, Lyndon Johnson promoted the Great Society, a package of social programs that included Medicare, federal aid for primary and secondary school education, the Model Cities Act, the War on Poverty, and various consumer protection and anticrime programs.

America has come through a revolution, a civil war, and two world wars. We have enabled many nations to freely choose their own form of government. We have sought to provide economic equality for all our people. We have survived, but only through borrowing and therefore increasing our national debt.

We must make no apologies for this debt. Not to be in debt today would be at the expense of our conscience and freedom. How honorable would our prosperity be if we did not share it with the less fortunate? How noble would our liberty be if we had turned our back on the injustices of Hitler? How honorable would our freedom be if we had turned a deaf ear to the cry from weaker nations threatened by oppressive powers? Let us credit our past administrations for rolling up a debt that is essentially honorable. We gave our best sons and daughters and incurred an incredible debt to help other people who spoke different languages, lived in diverse cultures, and embraced religions alien to our own.

The necessity and obligation of incurring our debt, however noble that may be, does not negate our responsibility to look critically at the obvious wasteful spending, mismanagement, and inefficiency our federal government has established as its trademark since the early 1930s. This government waste to the present day has contributed greatly to our ever-increasing federal debt. We must recognize these mistakes and inefficiencies and resolve them. We are not trying to fix the blame. We are trying to fix the problem!

In 1981, President Reagan appointed a special commission known as the Private Sector Survey on Cost Control. This commission was composed of 161 top executives, and it staffed thirty-six task forces at a cost of more than $75 million. All of this was paid by private companies at no cost to the government. The Private Sector Survey on Cost Control undertook a comprehensive, monumental task of assimilating data on wasteful government expenditures, program mismanagement, system failures, and overall inefficiency. After its three-year study, the commission produced approximately twenty-one thousand pages itemizing its findings. Nearly twenty-five hundred cost-cutting, revenue-enhancing recommendations were made that would save $424 billion in the first three years of implementation and would rise to more than $1.9 trillion each year by the year 2000.[8]

In a personal letter to the president, J. Peter Grace, the head of the commission, said, "If the American people realized how rapidly government spending is likely to grow under existing legislative programs, I am convinced they would compel their elected representatives to 'get government off their backs.'"[9] The commission found that if current wasteful government spending continues in future years, fiscal disaster is inevitable. In 1902 the government spent less than 10 percent of the national income. Since then, government spending has risen to 41 percent of the national income in 1980.

The letter to the president continued, "The project was structured and staffed to effect enduring improvement so that our children and grandchildren would not inherit a situation that would be devastating to them and on the values of our economic and social system."[10]

The facts are real and frightening as we come to understand the enormous burden the federal debt and deficits place upon our economy. The thought of what might face our children is even more frightening. We have been called the richest country in the world, a world economic leader. But we must ask ourselves if we are really so rich. If we are that wealthy, it is only because we are spending the money that rightly belongs to our children, grandchildren, and great-grandchildren. In reality we are poor. Our national debt threatens to impose a taxation without representation on future generations. Concerned citizens, including you, can make a difference and we will show you how.

Who Are We to Speak Up?

Why, you might ask, are a Protestant minister and a young businessman writing a book about the federal debt?

What credentials in economics can we marshal to gain credibility in dealing with this subject?

Some years ago I retained the noted architect Philip Johnson to design the Crystal Cathedral. His first set of drawings left me unenthused. He noticed the conspicuous lack of excitement within me. "Is something wrong?" he asked warily.

"Who am I to question the man who is the leading architect of our time?" I asked cautiously. I remember the scene vividly. His slender body was silhouetted against the east window of his thirty-fifth-floor office of the Seagram Building on Park Avenue.

His eyes focused firmly on mine as he admonished me, "Let's understand something right now, Dr. Schuller. Architecture is too important to leave to architects."

Encouraged and disarmed I blurted out my honest feelings. I said, "I love the glass roof in your plan, but the walls should be glass too."

He accepted my suggestion and went on to design the cathedral with glass walls as well as a glass ceiling. In retrospect I have come to believe that Philip Johnson was articulating a universal principle. Architecture is too important to leave to the architects. Likewise, religion is too important to leave to the theologians; science is too important to leave to the scientists; government is too important to leave to the politicians; peace is too important to leave to the diplomats; and economics is too important to leave to the economists.

Ultimately all disciplines must take into account the nature of the human being. Human values cannot be disregarded in any subject. Possibility thinking is the study of human development. It is intensely relevant to the subject of the national economy, for possibility thinking motivates human beings to tackle great problems with a positive mental attitude.

Possibility thinking asks challenging questions, such

as, What goals would you set for yourself if you knew you could not fail? And what decisions would you make if there were no outside forces to limit you? Possiblity thinking believes in managing by objectives. Creative leadership rather than crisis management naturally follows.

What is leadership? It is recognizing problems that exist today and problems that are sure to befall us if we neglect setting goals to prevent their outbreak in the future. To possibility thinkers, goals rise out of problems that call for resolution. Positive goals will prevent problems from occurring tomorrow. That's possibility-thinking leadership.

What the United States needs right now is possibility-thinking leadership to tackle the economic problems that face us today and will surely engulf us tomorrow.

Let us never forget that in a democracy, leadership is in the hands of the electorate. Leadership is the force that sets the goals. In a democracy, that force is offered to the people. The people, who will have to pay the bills and live with the results of the economic climate, must not surrender leadership of the economic situation to the economists. Ultimately, if our country dies from economic mismanagement or thrives with economic prosperity, the blame or credit will rest upon neither politicians nor economists but upon the consensus of the majority expressed at the ballot box. Therefore, we call upon all citizens of America to rise up and take command by demanding that our elected officials set goals that will guarantee the economic freedom of our unborn children and their children's children.

The time has come for the people of the United States of America to call for a declaration of economic independence. Let's unite to pay off the national debt ourselves and give our children and grandchildren the opportunity of enjoying the fruits of their labor and creativity.

How Can Anything Be Done?

How will we do it? Exactly the way we tackle and solve all other problems. By getting down to the ABCs of mountain moving, problem solving, success generating, possibility thinking. And what are these basics?

A—Attitude

Everything starts with an attitude. A negative attitude is certain to produce negative results. A positive attitude is certain to produce positive results.

Social philosopher George Herbert Mead suggested that attitude constitutes "the beginning of an act." He said,

> If one approaches a distant object, he approaches it with reference to what he is going to do when he arrives there. If one approaches a hammer he is muscularly ready to seize the handle of the hammer. The latter stages of the act are present in the early stages . . . in the same sense that they serve to control and process itself.[11]

According to Mead, an attitude is not simply a point of view, a static state of mind. It is an integral part of action, a determinant of the course and outcome of any human act. Your attitude governs the way you act, the way the action will unfold, and the consequences of action. What can come about from a positive attitude is clearly exciting!

The financial crisis facing our country demands that, as citizens, we should examine our personal attitudes toward the situation because it is our money the government is spending.

B—Belief

Impossible situations change permanently when a positive attitude evolves into belief. Negative thinkers say,

"I've got to see it before I believe it." The error in that attitude is obvious. The truth is, we've got to believe it before we see it. In every situation we have the freedom to choose what dreams we will believe in. Again and again the history of individuals, institutions, and nations proves the thesis that what we achieve depends on what we choose to believe.

C—Commitment

Possibility thinking moves mountains when a positive attitude produces a positive belief that evolves into a concrete commitment. Again and again in sports, in politics, in war and peace, success does not necessarily go to the most talented or to the wealthiest, but to those that are the most committed. There are no great people. The difference between the so-called great persons and nations and those of lesser rank is a matter of commitment. Great people simply make commitments to a greater goal. They dream nobler dreams. The greatest people in history are average people who have the commitment to tackle bigger problems than anyone else before them. The greatness of any generation will be molded and measured by the mountains it chooses to conquer.

D—Decisions

Possibility thinking works wonders because it is such a practical philosophy for creative decision making. In reality, problems are only decisions waiting to be made. I have counseled troubled persons with this honest evaluation: "You don't have a problem to solve, you simply have a decision to make!"

For more than thirty-five years I have applied the principles of possibility thinking to every conceivable problem short of erasing the national debt. Possibility thinkers are decisive leaders. Never do we surrender leadership to problems. We always let the positive, undeveloped possibilities call the shots. Never, then, do we let the problem-solving phase move into the decision-making phase. We make the right decisions simply because they are the right decisions, even if they appear to be impossible to carry out.

Again and again we see the miracle unfold. When the right decision is made in the face of impossible problems, the waters separate. Moses marches across the dry bottom of the Red Sea to the astonishment of the enemy behind him. The first step to paying off the national debt is to make a decision.

We can regain our true wealth as a nation only with a concentrated and deliberate commitment and decision to liquidate the debt we have accumulated during our first two hundred years.

Our Dream for America

We can be a debt-free nation by 2005. To be debt free would give us real wealth and real power: power to maintain our middle class; power to wipe out poverty; power to educate all citizens; power to expand our human values worldwide. Underdeveloped countries could have their potential developed through low-interest loans and investments from America. No longer a debtor, our country would become a lender once more at low interest rates to struggling people worldwide. The money that now goes to pay off the interest on the debt of the past two hundred years would instead spur economies around the world. Our children would know the power that comes with economic freedom.

As a nation, we have reached a time when we must grow up and face our responsibilities to pay off the federal debt. Then when we celebrate our 250th anniversary, the writers of history will declare that the greatest battle ever fought in our first 250 years was not the War of 1812, the

Civil War, World War I, or World War II. The biggest battle ever fought and won was the battle of the 1980s and 1990s when the people of the United States of America waged an all-out war to eliminate the federal debt and liberate the future generations!

2

There's a Crack in the Liberty Bell

In one form or another, debt reaches into the home of each person on earth, whether it is the international bank conglomerates transferring money via satellite from Zurich, Switzerland, to Johannesburg, South Africa, or the nomadic Bedouin shepherd in the Sinai desert trading goat skins for the promise of water rights from an oasis.

Carefully managed debt is essential to trade and commerce. From the very basic level to the most sophisticated technological currency transactions, debt is a part of everyday life. Whenever there is a transfer of goods and services to someone who agrees to pay in exchange for them, debt is incurred.

The flow of your earnings finances the debt on your house. In a similar way, the flow of the government's earnings through tax revenues and sales of treasury bonds, bills, and other financial instruments finances the federal debt.

Debt is an integral and vital part of our world's economic system. Much of the expansion the United States has enjoyed in the last two hundred years has been because our nation, corporations, and individuals have had the freedom and ability to borrow against their future productivity.

Few people will disagree that there are many times when it pays to go in debt, times when it is moral, honorable, and smart to incur debt, both individually and institutionally. Few of us, for instance, have the ability to pay cash for our homes, so we borrow the money and plan to pay the debt from future earnings.

However, the practice of financing our wants and needs through borrowed funds has become a national habit. But it all started when interest rates were relatively low. Thirty-year mortgages at 6 to 7 percent interest were common until the mid-1970s. Many enterprises correctly calculated that the cash flow derived from the sale of their goods and services could finance long-term, fixed-rate mortgages and still return a profit.

Many prudent investors and speculators have borrowed money to invest in prime parcels of land and have seen the value of their investments increase. Others have borrowed to buy gold at $35 an ounce. When gold skyrocketed to more than $800 an ounce, some investors received this investment back twenty times, more than enough to pay the interest on the borrowed money.[1]

It also makes sense to go in debt if you come across a once-in-a-lifetime opportunity. If you have a limited number of days, months, or years in which to take advantage of a passing opportunity and you have the cash flow to finance a mortgage, then you would be smart and responsible to incur a debt.

Many economists feel that debt is necessary and advantageous. For instance, our country suffered a terrible shock following that fateful day in October 1929 when the floor of the New York Stock Exchange was littered with worthless sell orders silently testifying to the unexpected crash of the stock market. Banks and private investors lost billions of dollars. Food lines and homeless people were a common scene in America's cities and countrysides. The jobless rate soared to crippling proportions. It was one of the darkest times in our nation's history.

But the theories of John Maynard Keynes were credited with pulling our nation out of this period of depression. He said it would be advantageous for our nation to go in debt in order to create jobs and opportunities. His basic credit-supply theory worked. America struggled to its feet by borrowing the money against future productivity.

But Keynes also formulated specific guidelines in the implementation of his theory which have gone unheeded by our nation: (1) never run a deficit in an expanding economy, and (2) repay the debt during a productive cycle. According to Keynes, to disregard either of these economic rules would bring on hyperinflation, recession, or depression.

Managed properly, debt can be a positive means to growth and productivity. But excessive debt and the resulting interest payments can be a strangling, crippling, restricting force. Debt can be draining not only financially but also emotionally.

I will never forget watching my father struggle under the heavy burden of debt he incurred.

Work was tough in northwest Iowa in the early 1900s. As a teen-ager, Anthony Schuller could find only a job as a hired hand doing manual farm chores. But he managed to save a dollar here and there until finally he took a chance on his dream. With all the courage he could muster, my father stepped into the office of the local banker. Land prices in the area had been rising steadily. As far as Dad could see, the value of an Iowa farm could only go up. The bankers thought so too. However, it was only a few short months before the Great Depression hit. Land prices plummeted. Dad looked back later and knew he "bought high," but he knew he could always draw from the soul of the earth to repay his mortgage.

Then the dust bowl years came. Suffering from the relentless drought, crops were wiped out. The raw produce Dad took to market was hardly enough to make the interest payments on his debt. He hoped and prayed for times to change, for miraculous record crops and all-time-high market prices for his eggs, milk, and hogs. Dad held on to his dream, knowing that in a few short years the payment of the principal on his mortgage would fall due.

Then another disaster hit.

It was late one summer when I was home from college. The clouds grew dark as the noise of thunder rumbled in the distance. Suddenly, out of the darkest cloud, a long, ballonlike cloud seemed to stretch out into a twisting snake. It was unmistakably a tornado.

"We're going to have to make a run for it, and fast!" Dad shouted. We quickly climbed into the car and headed out of the path of the tornado. From several miles away we watched the twisting funnel make its path across our farm.

After it had gone, we headed back down the familiar country roads. As we crested a small hill, we couldn't see the top of the barn that usually landmarked our farm. All nine farm buildings were gone. There was no rubble, only clean white foundation lines where the buildings once stood. The pedigree breeding bull walked dazed in the deserted farmyard. Somehow he survived even though the barn was dropped in splintered pieces a mile down wind. All of the horses were dead. The pigs were dead. The machinery was gone. The crops were cut off at the roots. Besides the bull, only the milk cows survived since they grazed in pastures outside the immediate path of the tornado.

My father's hand drew into a tight fist, and he beat the steering wheel and cried in agony to his wife. "It's all gone, Jennie. It's all gone!" The farm he nurtured, cultivated, and cared for all those years was sucked up in a matter of seconds. And the heavy mortgage he acquired years before would fall due in only three years. Everything he worked for was totally wiped out.

The insurance paid only $3,500. Sparing only a few

hundred dollars, Dad took the money to the bank. "Sir," he said to the banker, "I want to make a payment on my mortgage. It falls due in three years, you know. I counted on a good crop this year, but now that is gone. But I want you to know that I plan to pay off my debt. I can't lose my farm."

The banker was visibly impressed, especially when my father mapped out how he planned to keep farming without buildings or machinery. With $50 of the insurance money, Dad bought a dilapidated four-story house. Piece by piece, nail by nail, board by board we dismantled it and rebuilt our house. We even made a makeshift barn to protect the animals. The house was tiny and far less attractive than the one that was lost, but I'll never forget when my father said, "Well, at least the buildings are paid for!"

With renewed confidence the bankers extended my father's loan for another ten years. It was a moving moment when Dad came home that night and at the dinner table prayed, thanking God that he did not lose the farm.

I learned my first lesson about economics that summer. Debt is an oppressive burden when times are tough. And interest on the debt is the toughest and most thankless bill to pay.

Years later my father saved enough money so that he not only paid off his mortgage but also bought a small "luxury" house in the nearby town of Alton, Iowa. There he enjoyed the last years of life with the freedom that comes from being debt free. It is amazing how liberating that feeling was to my parents and is to those who experience it today. That freedom can be ours as a nation. Later we shall see how our society would be different and our standard of living improved if, as a nation, we would discover the power of being debt free.

The destructive force of excessive debt is not limited to individuals or corporations. The emotional and financial drain of being in debt is also felt at the national level.

Monumental debt has virtually destroyed the economies of thirteen Latin American countries. Their outstanding debt to United States banks totals over $800 billion. Mexico currently owes more than $98 billion to American banks. In 1982 it was the inability of the Latin American countries to pay their interest payments that sent shockwaves through the financial communities.[2]

In the mid-1970s, when the price of oil was skyrocketing, Mexico and other countries borrowed to develop their oil industries and tap their tremendous natural reserves. They felt they could produce a product that would appreciate in value faster than the cost of paying the interest on the debt. For a while they were right. But boom led to bust. Oil prices fell while interest rates went up. And the revenues from the oil industries could not meet the interest payment on the debt.

The American bankers kept saying, "Countries don't go bankrupt. Do they?" And they lent more billions of dollars to these countries so that they could meet their interest payments.

There is an old adage in financial circles that says if you owe the bank $10,000, you don't sleep at night. But if you owe the bank $1 million, the banker doesn't sleep at night.

This type of excessive debt reaches deeper than just into the financial elements of society. The psychological and social implications are equally damaging. In 1984, Bolivia announced that it refused to pay its $3.9 billion debt. This followed a 75 percent devaluation of the Bolivian peso and a 500 percent increase in sugar, bread, and gasoline prices. Bolivia's most powerful unions had marched in protest while thousands of citizens rioted in the streets.

Brazil tried to cope with its $96 billion debt by limiting salary increases while raising food and gasoline prices. It cut social welfare and aid to the country's main oil, electrical, and mining industries. Mass riots and looting of food stores in Rio de Janeiro and Sao Paulo quickly followed.

The harsh reality is that the excessive debt of the Latin American countries has crippled their economies and strapped the United States financially as well. As long as a person or a country is indebted, that entity is enslaved to the consequences of economic swings, such as when oil prices went down when they were expected to go up. The responsibility of paying off the debt still remains.

Financial crisis caused by excessive debt is not limited to foreign countries. In 1975 New York City ran out of money, effectively defaulted on its financial obligations, and was for all intents and purposes bankrupt. The city had built up a monumental debt of $13.6 billion! The day of reckoning finally came when interest payments on New York City's debt obligations could not be paid.

Major United States banks refused to underwrite and purchase New York City bonds which financed the city's debt. Mayor Abraham Beame appealed to the federal government's sense of loyalty for a bailout. He asked, "Would the French disown Paris? Would the Soviets abandon Moscow?" But the government could not establish a precedent for other cities to rely on in the future. President Ford declared, "If we go on spending more than we have, providing more benefits and more services than we can pay, then a day of reckoning will come to Washington and the whole country as it has to New York City. . . . When that day of reckoning comes, who will bail out the United States?"[3]

Debt holds hostage both the debtor and the creditor. Could the United States with its $1.836 trillion debt and yearly budget deficit of $165 billion be headed down the same path as many Latin American countries and New York City?

In 1972, when the national debt was $427 billion, the deficit was $23 billion, and interest payments on the debt were $21 billion, the *Los Angeles Times* printed an article suggesting ways to pay off the national debt. It was to be taken as a sophisticated joke because everyone knew the debt would take care of itself. People laughed. But now, more than one decade later, no one is laughing. Unconcerned smiles have been replaced by shocked, blank stares. How did it happen? How could the debt have grown so deep and so fast?

Some economists say the bulk of the debt is caused by excessive government spending. In the past ten years, government spending has increased dramatically. Others say a shortfall in tax revenues is the cause. Mismanagement and inefficiency are also considered to be causes. But one of the most important elements contributing to the rise in the federal debt is the *interest on the debt itself*. The Congressional Budget Office said that in 1984, $114 billion was paid in interest on the debt.[4]

Interest is the ultimate entitlement. It must always be paid, and it is the most unproductive outlay of money in the government's budget. It produces nothing.

For a nonprofit institution, such as the government, paying interest on borrowed money is not as advantageous as it is for the private sector which can borrow funds and deduct interest payments from income taxes. The federal government does not pay income taxes and therefore cannot deduct the interest.

The Congressional Budget Office estimates that interest payments on the debt will reach $195 billion by 1988.[5] It would seem that this would take more money out of the private sector, money that could be used otherwise to provide goods and services and stimulate our economy.

The government's borrowing to pay the interest on the debt reminds me of the one time when I had to borrow money for something that literally went up in smoke! In September 1950 I took my first job as pastor of a small

Government Expenditures Compared to Gross National Product

Dollars

(in billions)

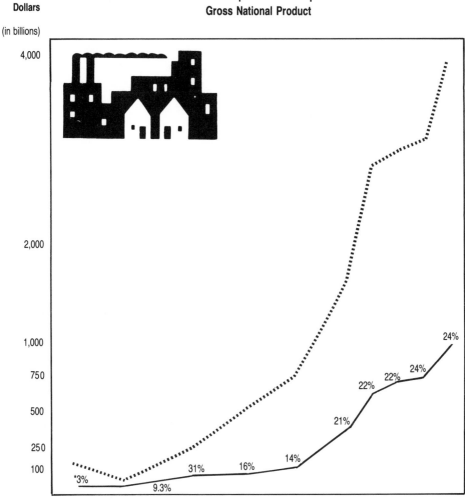

Fiscal Years

GNP ·········

GOVT. OUTLAYS————

Source for GNP: U.S. Dept. of Commerce, Bureau of Economic Analysis

Source for Expenditures: U.S. Treasury Dept; Annual Statement as taken from *World Almanac—1984*

*Expenditures as Percentage of GNP

church in Ivanhoe, Illinois. In addition to my $200-a-month salary, the church provided me with a parsonage. We had just moved in when I received a call from a church deacon. "Bob, I think you should order your coal."

"Coal?" I asked.

"Yes," he explained. "Your furnace in the parsonage is coal burning."

Then I remembered that I was responsible for all of my utilities. So I went to the local lumberyard where I was told I could order the coal. The manager greeted me enthusiastically and seemed to know exactly how much coal I needed: five tons at a total cost of $77.50.

"When can you deliver?" I asked.

"Tomorrow afternoon, if that is okay."

"That sounds great!" I said as I turned around to leave, my order complete.

"Oh, Reverend!" the manager called after me. "That will be $77.50, please!"

I stopped in my tracks. I assumed he would bill me. "But I don't have any money with me. Can't you bill me? I'd like to open a charge account anyway."

The decision was written all over the manager's face even before he spoke. "Sorry, Reverend. But we don't deliver any coal unless it is paid for in advance." He went on to explain. "Your coal bin is in the basement, right? Well, if we deliver the coal and dump it in the basement, and you don't pay the bill, it's a heck of a job trying to haul it out. If you want a loan, you'll have to go to the bank."

Somewhat taken aback, I left the lumberyard and headed straight to the First National Bank. There the manager greeted me warmly, saying he had heard good things about me. Finally, he leaned back in his chair and asked, "What can I do for you, Reverend?"

"I am here to borrow $75, sir," I said unashamedly.

"What do you want to borrow the money for? Whether I loan it to you or not depends on what you plan to do with it."

I knew I had an unbeatable cause. My needs were beyond debate. On top of that, I was a distinguished citizen of the community. Without any reservation, I dropped my request. "I want to borrow the money to buy my winter supply of coal. I need five tons and the going rate is . . ."

"Wait a minute, Reverend!" he quickly interrupted. The smile was gone. A firm, tough, business look replaced the sparkle in his eye. "Reverend, we never loan money to buy coal!" The words were spoken with final authority.

I couldn't believe what I was hearing. He must have read my perplexity because he went on to explain his position.

"You must understand something about banks. The money we have to loan is not our money. Hard-working people put their savings here. They trust us to use their money to make money for them. We cannot lose their money. Therefore, we can't loan money without collateral."

"Collateral?" I asked, totally ignorant. "What's that?"

"Collateral," he said with a smile, "is when you have something of value to offset the debt. If you borrow money for a house or a car and can't make the payments, we simply take the car or house and sell it. We pay ourselves back, and any surplus is yours. That's called your equity. But if you borrow money to buy coal, the coal cannot be collateral because you will burn it in the furnace. Then if you don't pay your bill, our customers will lose their savings. Their money will literally go up in smoke! My advice to you, Reverend, is run your personal and church business so that you never need to borrow money for coal."

The banker must have sensed my panic. "I will tell you what I will do," he said with a look of mercy. "If I loaned

you $75, could you pay it back in five monthly payments of
$15 each? There will be interest added on top of that, of
course."

"Oh, yes!" I said with a sigh of relief. "I can make
those payments. There's no problem there at all."

"Good. Then we have a deal," the banker said with a
smile as he shuffled some papers in front of me to sign.

As I got ready to leave, check in hand, the banker
stood to shake my hand. His eyes met mine. "Reverend,"
he said seriously, "remember, never again borrow money
for coal."

I walked out of that bank with a $75 check and one of
the most important economic lessons of my life. Never
again would I borrow money for something that could not be
held as collateral or that would not produce a product or
service that would grow and appreciate in value. It is safe to
say that most, if not all, of our $1.836 trillion federal debt is
for "coal money" and it has all been burned up! Bullets,
obsolete equipment, salaries of federal employees, social
security, payments on the interest on the national debt—all
of this is coal money.

Every year our government borrows money to pay the
interest on the national debt. It is like burning that coal in
my furnace. Borrowing money to pay the interest on the
debt is simply fueling our debt because we are not paying off
the principal. Rather, we are adding to it. Perhaps the only
difference between my borrowing money for the coal and
the government's borrowing for the interest on the debt is
that my monthly payment was only $15. The federal govern-
ment pays $9.5 billion a month!

Have you ever stopped to think about what could be
done with $9.5 billion a month? $114 billion a year? What if
our nation did not have a debt? Is such a situation possible?

To find out, we asked the Hudson Institute, a nonprofit

public policy research organization, to study the costs, benefits, and plausibility of a fiscal strategy that would eliminate the federal debt. The results were unexpected. The implications were more serious than either we or the institute had anticipated.

A paper prepared by Dr. Arnold H. Packer under the direction of Jim Wheeler, director of economic studies of the Hudson Institute, states that it is both wise and possible to first eliminate the federal deficit and then run sufficient budget surpluses to reduce and eliminate the debt.

According to the paper, "The benefits of reducing or eliminating the debt are great. The dangers of doing nothing are monumental" (see Appendix II). By the year 2000, we will be forced into severe fiscal discipline to avert disaster. If such a program were started now, fifteen years earlier, the nation would be measurably better off by the beginning of the next century, says the institute's report.

In preparing his study, Dr. Packer assumed three scenarios: (1) the debacle, (2) muddling through, and (3) debt elimination. In each case a twenty-year projection was made, until 2005.

The choice is ours as to which path our great country will follow!

The worst and most fearful of the three scenarios painted by the Hudson Institute is the *debacle scenario*. In this case, the government deficits will remain at a constant $45 billion per year, *exclusive of interest on the national debt*. The total deficit will grow each year by the amount of increase in interest on the national debt. This $45 billion deficit is called the "program deficit." Such a scenario has the effect of adding $45 billion plus the interest on the national debt to the principal owed on the debt each year.

According to the report, our country's financial situation will be completely unstable under this scenario. And yet the Congressional Budget Office estimates just such a $45 billion program deficit per year for the rest of the decade!

Financial projections under this scenario are pointless because the situation cannot continue until 2005. Interest on a debt of $43.7 trillion in 2005 would equal 34 percent of the gross national product. This is more than the entire income of the federal government! The annual deficit, by 2000, would be three times as great as American profits instead of two-thirds as great as it was in 1984. This clearly presents an impossible situation!

FISCAL SITUATION IN 2000 AND 2005

Scenario	(Deficit) or Surplus	Interest on Debt	Program (Deficit) or Surplus
		($ billions)	
2000			
Debacle	(3160)	3115	(45)
Muddling	(240)	440	200
Debt Red.	230	70	300
2005			
Debacle	(9545)	9500	(45)
Muddling	(230)	540	310
Debt Red.	0	0	0

The deficits will continue to grow due to the increasing interest payments. Eventually bondholders who finance the debt will lose confidence in the dollar and America's capacity to meet its obligations. When confidence is lost, investors will rush to sell their bonds and notes at a discount. America will be faced with a financial and economic crisis. Banks will fail and credit will be abruptly restricted. This crisis will not be limited to the United States but will lead to severe worldwide recession.

The startling fact is that this tragedy does not depend on a spending spree in Washington, but on government's continuing to run a deficit at the level that the Congressional

Budget Office projects for the rest of the decade! Avoiding this scenario will require a concentrated effort on the part of the American people!

The second scenario, called the *muddling through scenario,* assumes just that. America will barely be able to muddle through the financial mess it will find itself in. The reason? Too little action too late!

Under this scenario, budget deficits would be kept in the $200 to $300 billion range, which is a diminishing percentage of the increasing gross national product. To achieve even this modest action, however, will require painful fiscal discipline. This plan also idealistically assumes that there will be no recessions or significant interest rate increases.

The growing interest payment on the debt will eat away at the government's capacity to perform. To muddle through in 2005, the government will have to take in $310 billion more than it spends on programs to cover part of the $540 billion interest payment on a $5.9 trillion debt. And this still leaves a $230 billion budget deficit!

Under this scenario, our government will have to take in a program surplus of $300 billion by 2005 just to keep the deficit at $230 billion. If this surplus is not achieved, we will quickly find ourselves in the disaster of the previous scenario.

At some point, we need to begin to repay our debt. By

SITUATION IN YEAR 2005

Scenario	Debt $Trillion	Deficit $Billion	Debt/GNP %	Interest/GNP	
				% in 2005	% in 2008
1. Debacle*	43.7	9545	257	56	96
2. Muddling Through	5.9	230	33	3	0
3. Eliminate Debt	0	0	0	0	0

*Assuming a 50 basis point increase in real (and nominal) interest rates annually.

2005, we will need a program surplus of $300 billion just to avoid disaster. But if we begin today to create a surplus of the same amount, we could eliminate the debt by the year 2005. Then we will know the power of being debt free at the beginning of the next century!

The *debt-elimination scenario* is the most promising forecast, but it requires belt tightening now. Revenues must be increased or spending decreased by $10 billion per year for the next fifteen to twenty years. Under this plan, the $45 billion program deficit must be eliminated by the year 1986 and the total federal deficit eliminated by 1991. As a result, the entire debt will be paid off by 2005!

The revenue increases required to achieve this are not great: only 5 percent for individuals and 15 percent for corporations. Moreover, these increases would be phased in gradually. In addition, the money supply must grow 1 or 2 percent more rapidly each year than it would under the muddling-through scenario.

In the short run, this plan would mean we would each have less money to spend, averaging $350 to $400 less per family per year. This would come from increased taxes coupled with reduced interest income from declining interest rates. But the reason for decrease is obvious. As a country we would be paying off our debt.

In spite of the immediate reduction, we will all become better off financially in the long run. Interest rates would fall to 8-9 percent. The nation's economic structure would be more productive. Investment productivity, exports, economic output, and housing stock would be higher. Small businesses and state and local governments would have less difficulty borrowing, and the debt-ridden Third World countries would have an easier time paying off their loans.

By 2005 the federal debt would be wiped out. A substantial tax reduction would also be in order!

What would a debt-free economy mean to you and me?

Projected Figures for Moody's Corporate Bond Rate
According to Three Scenarios

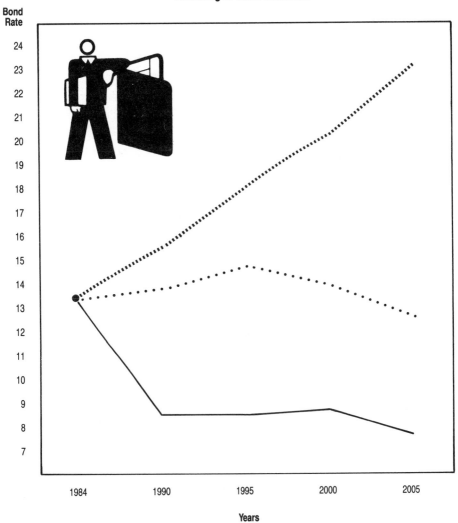

Debacle ••••••••

Muddling Through • • • • •

Debt Reduction ————

To your children and my children? A debt-free economy would affect every area of our lives, but let's look closely at the area of housing.

In 1984 the mortgage payment necessary to finance an average mortgage in the United States at 14 percent on the average house with a price of $100,000 and a loan of $80,000 was $947.90 per month, or $11,374.80 per year. Since the average family earns about $20,000 annually, home ownership is not within reach of that family. But if mortgage rates were 7 percent instead of 14 percent, the monthly payment on that same loan would be $532.25—or $6,387 per year—putting home ownership within the reach of millions more families. What would that do to the economy?

To begin with, the lumber industry in the forests of Washington would go back to full employment. Glass factories in Ohio, carpet manufacturers in the Deep South, and aluminum and steel factories in the East would all find orders pouring in. Factories for small appliances for kitchens and bathrooms would be superproductive. Companies that make boxes for shipping anything from light bulbs to plumbing fixtures would have "Help Wanted" signs hanging out front. The boom in our productivity would be fantastic! Plus, our children and grandchildren could dream of owning their own home and paying it off in their lifetime.

If America will decide to eliminate its national debt, it will have the financial power to provide homes for all people and in the process build the economic foundations for the continuation of a strong and productive future. No longer will our country be laden with the emotional and financial burden of debt. Rather, it will be a country that knows the liberating power of being debt free!

3

Why Has Nothing Been Done?

We arrived at the warehouse of Fleetwood Enterprises where we were to meet John Crean, founder and chief executive officer of America's leading manufacturer of motor-homes, travel trailers, and manufactured housing. We knew he had built his company on a no-debt policy. Curious to learn more, we arranged to meet him for lunch.

John's wife, Donna, greeted us and took us down a hallway to a room where we could find her husband. We expected to see an office with a large desk. Instead the room was a garage. Covered with sawdust, John stopped his work on a new, experimental recreational vehicle. Over a sandwich at a nearby coffee shop, he shared his story with us.

"I started in 1950 making venetian blinds for trailers. But at the time I couldn't get any credit. I had very little credit before I started the company, and what I did have was bad because I had been late on payments. So I was forced to operate on a cash basis. I bought parts for cash and I sold only for cash. I extended no credit. My sales policy was simply to give a lower price for a better quality product. Well, I was into the business less than a year when my major competitor filed for bankruptcy. It turned out that when I started dealing on a cash basis, he ended up with all the bad credit accounts, all the deadbeats."

Shortly afterward, John began to manufacture travel trailers, and he was extended credit from many of his suppliers. "But I didn't like it," he said. "I kept careful records so as not to miss a payment." As business volume increased so did his credit, and so did the credit he extended to his customers.

But then the recession in 1954 hit. Suddenly he couldn't collect his receivables, which meant he didn't have his payables. "I had $300,000 due to me in receivables, but I owed the same in payables," John recalled. "Since I couldn't pay my bills, there was a total shutdown in deliveries. When you are in debt, you depend on your customers to pay their bills so that you can pay yours. If you have too many unpaid receivables, you can't extend more credit and you can't sell your product. Then you're in trouble. It was a terribly discomforting situation."

Determined to work things out, John took out a $10,000 loan from the bank to pay his bills. But before his checks cleared, the bank nervously recalled its money. "I had prided myself in never having a check bounce," said John. "Now they all bounced. I decided then and there *never* to go in debt again, not even for one quarter. It was really a simple decision. Since then I have always bought and sold for cash."

Nine months later John was operating again on a no-debt policy. "Any economist will tell you that you can't do that in our economy and grow. All I can tell you is that it worked. In 1973, when the oil crisis hit America, the recreational vehicle industry was severely affected. Sales dropped off 75 percent. But because Feetwood was a debt-free corporation, we survived while other's didn't. When the crisis ended, there was a pent-up demand for R.V.'s. We came out that year with the same profitability as every other year."

Today, Fleetwood Enterprises is the leading manufacturer of motor-homes, travel trailers, and manufactured houses with sales in 1983 of more than $1.4 billion.

John's no-debt policy is not limited to his business. He and his wife have never had a mortgage and have always paid cash for their homes. "When you can't borrow money, and you see a goody you want, you know you can't have it unless you earn it. That gives you tremendous motivation to work. In 1951 my wife and I lived on a tight budget, but we always had a little left over. One day I saw this beautiful Jaguar XJ 120. Suddenly I wanted every extra bit of work I could get just to make an extra buck to buy that car. I had it in less than eighteen months."

John Crean feels that a no-debt policy would greatly benefit the United States also. As he found with his business, he believes paying off the national debt begins with making a decision.

"I would like to see the leadership emerge that would make paying off the national debt as much a priority as winning World War II was. If everyone would produce more, tighten their belts, we could pay it off. It might hurt a bit, but if it's a national priority, it will be a pretty short-term thing. To get it done it might take some pain and some long, hard work. But I'm willing to do it. I'll be the first to jump in!"

There can be little doubt that the rising federal debt is one of our nation's greatest national problems. Then why has nothing been done about it? Why don't we hear more about it? We hear about the deficits and the need for balanced budgets, but rarely do we hear about the deeper, underlying problem of the structural debt. Why don't our highest elected officials in both Congress and the executive branch of government decide to tackle this problem? Where are the voices of concerned citizens rallying together to speak out against this tyranny?

- **Is it possible that little action has been taken because people are not aware?**
- **Or because they simply do not care?**
- **Or because they don't dare?**

Is it possible that we are not aware of the enormity of our nation's debt? Do we really care about the ensuing consequences if nothing is done about it? Even if we are aware and care, do we dare tackle a problem that seems so imposing?

Are we aware of the difference between the country's budget deficit and the structural debt?

The news is filled with stories about the rising budget deficit. The deficit was a major point of debate in the 1984 presidential election. But what about the debt? Why are the print and electronic media virtually silent on the underlying debt?

An annual deficit of $164.5 billion is staggering, but that just represents an annual addition to the national debt, which is more than eleven times the size of the 1984 deficit. We need to understand that the underlying structural debt is the major cause of continuing yearly deficits. Budget deficits of any size increase the debt. And the interest on the debt remains a major cause of the budget shortfalls. With a $1.836 trillion debt, the interest payments equal $114.3 billion a year. In 1984, we paid $217,000 per minute simply to pay the interest on the debt! We need to know what the problem is before we can expect to discover the solution.

Are we, the American public, aware of the severity of our structural debt? Can we relate to the figure $1.836 trillion?

Jim Wheeler, a top economist for the Hudson Institute, explained to us that as he travels around the country to lec-

Dollars
(Thousands)

Federal Deficit

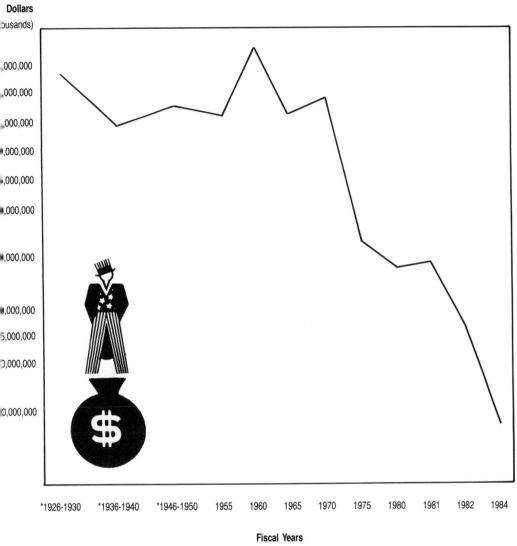

,000,000

,000,000

,000,000

,000,000

,000,000

,000,000

,000,000

,000,000

5,000,000

),000,000

),000,000

*1926-1930   *1936-1940   *1946-1950   1955   1960   1965   1970   1975   1980   1981   1982   1984

Fiscal Years

*(yearly average)

ture on the budget deficit and the national debt, he has tremendous interest and concern from his audience until he gives the hard facts. As soon as he writes on the blackboard or overhead screen the figure $1,836,000,000,000 (by the way, this is not a typographical error—every zero belongs here), his listeners get what he calls the "eglo" syndrome; that is, their eyes glaze over.

The $1.836 trillion debt has an unreal quality about it to all of us. We cannot comprehend this staggering amount, especially when the average American family income is only $20,000 per year. It might help to realize that $1.836 trillion amounts to a $7,714 debt for every person—not every family, but every person—in America.

Are we aware of our country's hidden debts? Are we being told the whole truth about our nation's financial picture?

Apparently not. With an ingenious stroke of the pen, our government has hidden much of our nation's true debt with an attractive accounting device. For example, unfunded social security payments which amount to more than $3 trillion are not included in statements that are released to Congress and the public as part of our accumulated debt.

High-risk loans and subsidies to special interest groups are also not included in the outstanding debt. This is called "off-budget lending," which means such figures do not appear on the budget sheets as amounts that contribute to the budget deficit. In 1974, Congress created the Federal Finance Bank, which in the last ten years has made loans totaling $1 trillion to subsidize everything from energy costs for certain segments of the country to small business loans and much more.

Rather than show up on the yearly budget deficits, this $1 trillion debt is entered into the Treasury Department's books and is sold to the public in the form of treasury securities. Although it is not paid for through taxes, this debt is unknowingly financed by people who purchase treasury bills and bonds. The danger is that this takes money out of our economy which could otherwise be used to repay the national debt or enable our economy to expand.

Estimates of our nation's debt, including these "hidden debts," range from $3.9 trillion to $12.8 trillion, depending on how conservative or liberal the interpretation might be. The National Taxpayers Union, for instance, says that the total federal debt is $12.237 trillion, which, assuming there are 80 million taxpayers, amounts to $152,967 of debt per taxpayer. If the Federal Finance Bank's debt and other hidden debts were included in our national debt, at least we would be aware of the problem. But now it is buried beneath a stack of accounting papers, hidden from our eyes, yet costing each one of us.

Are we aware of how we pay for the debt in our everyday lives through inflation?

The average American family pays $3,500 in federal government taxes each year, but these taxes currently finance less than 58 percent of our government's spending needs. Therefore, the government must raise money from other sources, which include sales taxes, customs duties, import taxes, corporate taxes, and a hidden tax called inflation. Inflation is one way we all pay for the debt. The National Taxpayers Union has drafted the statement of account on page 64 showing the actual liability of each United States taxpayer.

The government has seemed to prefer inflation, a subtle form of taxation, for the past ten years. By printing money, the government is able to make up the shortfall in tax revenues needed to pay its bills. But the result is the devaluation of every dollar in proportion to the amount of

STATEMENT OF ACCOUNT   **TERMS:**
You just keep paying

YOUR ATTENTION IS DIRECTED TO AMOUNTS DUE AS INDICATED BELOW:

DEBT OR LIABILITY ITEM	FEDERAL OBLIGATIONS	YOUR SHARE*
Public Debt	$ 1,490,000,000,000	$ 18,625
Accounts Payable	192,385,000,000	2,405
Undelivered Orders	480,450,000,000	6,006
Long Term Contracts	26,010,000,000	325
Loan and Credit Guarantees	553,254,000,000	6,916
Insurance Commitments	2,338,658,000,000	29,233
Annuity Programs	7,086,000,000,000	88,575
Unadjudicated Claims: International Commitments & Other Contingencies	70,567,000,000	882
TOTAL	$12,237,324,000,000	$152,967

*Based on 80 million real taxpayers. Reprinted by Permission

money printed by the Treasury Department. When the government prints too much money, our dollars buy less. As the Nobel-Prize-winning economist Milton Friedman said, "Who do you suppose pays for the deficit? There is no Dutch uncle. Not even an Uncle Sam to pay it. We all pay it, one way or another."[1]

It is much easier for members of the House or the president to turn to inflation as a means of raising funds rather than to declare outright that the government should raise taxes. Would you vote for someone who said, "I am going to raise your taxes by 50 percent"? But that is exactly what has happened. In the last ten years the purchasing power of the dollar has eroded.

Although inflation is currently under control, many economists feel that it could come roaring back at any time. Some estimates are that if the deficit is not reduced, inflation could shoot up to an annual rate of 16 percent. (We must not forget that inflation was about 14 percent between 1976 and 1980 before the deficit quadrupled.) Are we aware that at an annual rate of 16 percent inflation, our 1985 dollar

The Federal Budget
(Actual and Projected)

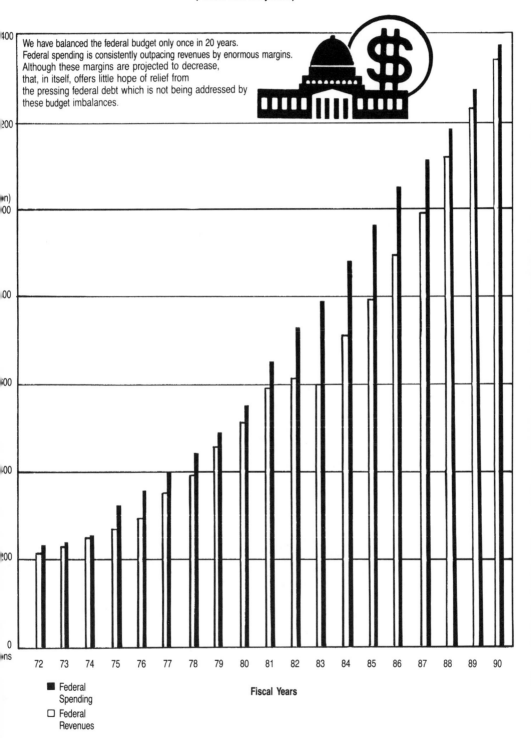

We have balanced the federal budget only once in 20 years.
Federal spending is consistently outpacing revenues by enormous margins.
Although these margins are projected to decrease,
that, in itself, offers little hope of relief from
the pressing federal debt which is not being addressed by
these budget imbalances.

72 73 74 75 76 77 78 79 80 81 82 83 84 85 86 87 88 89 90

■ Federal
　Spending
□ Federal
　Revenues

Fiscal Years

bill will be worth less than eleven cents in the year 2000?
Everyday costs would be at unthinkable levels. Some projected costs appear in the following list:

	1985	2000
New home	$100,000.00	$927,000.00
New car	$9,000.00	$83,400.00
Cart of groceries	$120.00	$1,112.00
Gallon of gas	$1.25	$11.59
Pack of cigarettes	$1.10	$10.20
Loaf of bread	$0.93	$8.62

Inflation is the most insidious tax of all, for it hits not only
the upper and middle classes, but also the poorest of the
poor.

Are we aware of the dangers of a growing federal debt?

Debt can throw a country into deep recession or depression or send it into an upward spiral of inflation. Rather
than choose depression, our government will probably
choose to print money and cripple us with inflation if
nothing is done about the debt. It is even possible for our
country to experience inflation and depression at the same
time, accompanied by high interest rates and a devaluation
of the dollar.

Other countries with large debts have suffered greatly
because of their inability to pay off their debts. Imagine that
you are walking through a supermarket doing your weekly
shopping. You wheel your cart down the aisles, carefully
choosing items with the most value per dollar. You are extremely price conscious. You are on a budget and have decided to bring only the money allocated for groceries with
you.

You choose a half-gallon of milk priced at $1.01. You
select a carton of eggs marked 69¢. A pound of ground beef
costs $1.29. After filling your cart, you push it to the front
checkstand where you are suddenly confronted by the assistant manager hovering over your basket of goods. He be-

gins to mark up the prices. Your milk is marked up to $1.26. Your eggs are upped to 81¢. Your beef now costs $1.61. All of your items are marked up 25 percent! The assistant manager says, "You know why we are doing this, don't you? The government has just devalued the dollar by 25 percent."

Does this sound unthinkable? Impossible? Do you believe it could never happen? It did. We had this experience last year on a trip to Israel! But it was not the first time it happened in that country. Nor is this scenario confined to Israel alone. Mexico, Argentina, and other countries have resorted to this method of dealing with inflation that is out of control.

Are we, the American public, aware that we have the ability to do something to solve the problem of our national debt?

So often when we hear of economic problems and government decisions, we close our ears and eyes. Our vision is confined to our small, private worlds. We tend to take the attitude that we can do nothing about it. But let us never forget that we live in a democratic society that depends on our involvement. The solutions to our problems are not in the government's hands, but in our hands.

There is a delightful story of a young boy and his friends who decided to try to trick the wise old man who lived in town. They caught a bird, and one boy held the bird tightly in his hand. He said to his friends, "I will ask the old man whether the bird is dead or alive. If he says the bird is dead, I will open my hand and let the bird fly away. But if he says the bird is alive, I will crush the bird until it is dead." And so the boys went to see the wise old man. "Is the bird dead or alive?" the boy asked. The wise old man looked down at the boy and thought a minute, then finally said, "The answer to that, my friend, is in your hands."

The answer to our country's debt problem is in our

hands. But we must first be aware of what the problem is. We need to understand the severity of a debt of $1.836 trillion. We must be informed about the hidden debts our government does not readily disclose to us. And we must become educated about how we pay for this debt through taxes and inflation in our everyday lives.

The fact that we are not aware is not the only reason why nothing has been done about the rising federal debt. Is it possible that many who are aware simply do not care? The reasons why we do not care provide an interesting insight into our society's lifestyles and values.

Do we care if we repay our debt?

I will never forget a unique visit I once had with a dear friend, the late Congressman Clyde Doyle. Clyde was one of the most distinguished representatives, having served in the United States Congress for more than twenty-five years. He was held in the utmost respect by Democrats and Republicans alike. I remember asking his advice about debt. Our church was still very young, and we had devised a long-term plan to go in debt to acquire land, buildings, and equipment to perform our services as a church. I calculated that the church would grow enough so that we could repay our debt over a twenty-year period. I felt we had to. I am convinced that it was this attitude of planning to pay off our debt that has enabled us to be a debt-free church today. I mentioned to Clyde, "We are planning to pay off our debt in twenty years. We feel this would be financially responsible. Do you agree?"

"Of course," he said.

"Okay," I ventured. "Then let me ask you how many years the federal government plans to take to repay its debt?"

I will never forget the look on his face and his answer. "Why, we will never pay off the debt, Bob." As he saw my stunned and confused expression, he went on to explain.

"You see, the federal government has no life span. As individuals, we all have a life span, and we have to think in terms of paying off our debt in our life spans. Otherwise our children will inherit a terrible liability, or we will face bankruptcy as old persons when we are incapable of earning more money. So as individuals, we have to think in terms of repaying the debt in twenty to thirty years. But our government expects to stay in business forever. So we never have to pay off the debt. All we do is pay the interest on the debt and keep refinancing it. We simply roll the debt over."

Is it possible that nothing has been done about the debt because we do not care if we ever repay it? We are glad to report that at least in Congress this attitude seems to be changing. No longer are senators and representatives suggesting that we only refinance the debt. As we prepared this book we contacted every senator and representative to find out how many share Clyde Doyle's viewpoint. Of more than 250 responses we received, only three persons agreed with rolling the debt over. The rest shared our concern that the debt is a problem that must be dealt with in our life span, not simply passed on to future generations.

Do we care enough to take the long look?

Is it possible that we do not care because we have no sense of history? We live in "the disposable age." We are the "throw-away generation." We live in "the instant culture." We buy disposable items. We bring in sod for an instant lawn. We import full-grown olive grees for a big show. Expediency is a plight that erodes the quality of leadership. We want it now and have forgotten the power of patience.

We need to learn the lessons of history. Quality takes time. All the money in the world cannot produce instant roses. Nature takes time for the rose plant to grow and the bud to form. Don't try to chemically or artificially produce a premature blossoming of a bud!

Too often companies have sacrificed actions that would result in stable, long-term growth on the altar of needing to report short-term, quarterly profits to the financial community. Such an attitude hurts the company, its employees, and its stockholders in the long run. Our country must also begin to think in terms of long-term financial responsibility, not just in terms of how much we can spend before the next election. When we talk about paying off the national debt in twenty to thirty years, the benefit to you and me may seem to be too far away. The truth is, the stimulation from the expectation is as exciting as the reality of that goal! The anticipation of going to a party is as satisfying as the party itself. I get terribly excited knowing that one day the palm trees I have planted will be one hundred feet tall. As possibility thinkers, we must anticipate what our country will be like when it is debt free twenty to thirty years from now. Then we will find the energy and excitement to actualize it.

We need to practice the "ABCs of possibility thinking": attitude, belief, and commitment. Then in 2005, the United States can be the financial powerhouse of the world! Just think what tremendous excitement and anticipation that will create. It is far easier to get excited about our country's strong financial future than its coming doom. It's like comparing plastic to marble, Formica laminated plastic to solid wood. The laminated plastic dulls and chips, but the wood can be sanded down and refinished to last hundreds of years.

Integrity and quality take time. America needs to take the long look to secure its financial future.

Do we care enough to give up our selfish interests for the sake of our children's future?

Debt is the subtlest form of immorality if it only serves our own selfish indulgences and willfully passes the obligation on to others. When we take something from others without their permission, that is stealing. If we ask our government to provide a product or a service for our own pur- poses, no matter how legitimate, knowing that the government will never be able to repay it in our lifetime and that the bill will be passed to our grandchildren with interest and that our children will pay our debt through taxes and inflation, are we are not taking from their income in ad- vance? Is that not stealing? When we run up a huge debt and have no plan to repay it, both the voters and those elec- ted form a silent conspiracy to steal from the next genera- tion.

Do we care enough to stop our elected officials from running up a debt that will pay for our pet projects?

How much of our debt has been incurred by elected officials whose primary purpose was their own election? If we citizens do not hold ourselves responsible to repay our debt, we open the door for opportunistic politicians to get elected on the promise of paying for our projects and needs. Unless we care about the debt, we cannot expect our elec- ted officials to care either. Perhaps some day we can elect officials who ask for our votes, even if they cannot promise us what we want because they will not ask our unborn grandchildren to pay for our indulgences.

Democracy can only survive when men and women of honor run for office on honorable promises. And democ- racy can only survive when we as citizens, with an equal sense of honor, refuse to make selfish and unreasonable de- mands upon our elected officials.

The responsibility falls on both the candidates and the public. President John F. Kennedy said it so well: "Ask not what your country can do for you; ask what you can do for your country."[2]

We have entered a critical time in history when we must stop asking our senators and representatives for per- sonal financial favors. Rather, we must ask them to tell us what we can do to pull our way out of this financial trap and into a powerful future for peace, freedom, and justice world-wide. The time is coming when a senator, representative, or president will be elected when he or she promises to reduce the national debt and never increase it beyond our ability to repay it over a predetermined number of years.

Many people in America do care. One man told us, "If it means that I have to take a cut in my social security check, I'm willing." Many young people are already planning to achieve financial security so that they will never need to make demands upon their government. They plan to become part of the solution, not part of the problem.

If we are governed by greed and care only for our-selves, rather than having a sense of shared community re-sponsibility, we must question whether democracy can survive generation after generation. If our democracy sur-vives only by people being elected to office based on our selfish demands, then the debt will continue to increase. Unless our hearts shift from "let the country help us," to "let us help our country," there will be no lasting freedom.

Do we care how our government spends the money we have entrusted to it?

Some of our elected officials don't care about the debt, and their attitude shows in their legislation. Not only do they spend money for projects that will aid them in their re-election, but many also do not give careful consideration to the financial aspects of more legitimate projects. Fiscal irre-sponsibility in the spending of our hard-earned tax dollars blatantly denies their concern about the debt. A classic ex-ample occurs when Congress passes bills to fund projects that it can never hope to complete.

Consider a problem that concerns all of us—mass transportation. Anyone caught in a traffic jam knows a problem exists. The temptation is to let the government pay for the solution. This may have to be the case, but consider how it has been approached so far.

In 1982, Congress established the Urban Mass Transit Administration (UMTA) which had the specific task of examining the feasibility of federally funded mass transportation systems in thirty cities. The UMTA was allocated $1.2 billion with the stipulation that no projects could be started unless the completion costs were known and the appropriate funds were available to complete them. Furthermore, the goal for these transportation systems was to meet the needs of lower income families.

During 1983, the entire $1.2 billion was distributed among only twelve cities instead of thirty as originally planned. Construction and improvements were begun. However, the administrator of UMTA, Ralph Stanley, estimated that at least $5 billion should be committed to these twelve projects.[3]

Congress will either have to appropriate more funds or scrap these projects in the middle of their progress. UMTA also estimates that the average fare for these systems will be seventy-five cents, which is forty-five cents higher than that charged by existing transit systems in the same cities. The people who the projects were originally intended to help will have to pay more than they are paying now.

Legislation was passed to meet the transportation needs of thirty cities, but the costs for only twelve cities is four times the entire amount of money allocated. How much more money will be poured into these projects when the other eighteen cities want their share? The increased cost is even higher when the interest this will add to the federal debt is included!

The fiscal irresponsibility of allocating money in this way leads us to question whether we really care about how our tax dollars are being spent. We don't care enough when we deceive ourselves about the costs and practicality of such projects.

Do we care enough to recognize that the problem is not going to go away by itself?

Hard as it is to believe, many people do not feel the debt is a problem. They feel that the productivity of future generations will be so strong that tax revenues resulting from the increased productivity will provide enough money to reduce the debt.

A prime example of this is the August 1984 Congressional Budget Office (CBO) report. The CBO estimates that in 1989 the budget deficit will be $289 billion, reflecting a growth over the next five years of only $124 billion from the current $165 billion deficit. However, the credibility of CBO projections can be questioned when we recall how inaccurate the CBO was in forecasting the deficits from 1982 to 1984. It projected a total shortfall over the three-year period of $273 billion. In fact, the true figure totalled $481 billion, 76 percent over projection.

This margin of error took place during one of the strongest economic recoveries of the century. GNP rose at an annualized rate of 9.5 percent during the first quarter of 1984, twice as much as projected. When growth in GNP was more than double projections and the deficit still grew nearly twice as much as was projected, how can we believe that growth in GNP alone will ever pay for our increased federal deficits, let alone the debt? Unless we really care about the debt to the point that we make clear-cut goals to reduce it, it will continue to grow in astronomical proportions.

We need to care about our economic future. If we don't care, who will? We need to care enough to take the long look, to face the fact that if nothing is done about it, the debt will eventually cripple our country's economic freedom. We need to care more about our children's future than our own selfish interests. And we need to care enough to ensure that every dollar spent in government today is being used wisely and efficiently.

If our future generations could speak, what would they say? Would they care? In a small corner of Virginia, a group of sixth graders studying government financing care about their future. Every week, the members of the class pool their allowances to mail $35 to Washington with a note that reads, "Help save America for us!"

To solve the problem of our national debt, we must first become aware of the magnitude of the situation. That awareness must make us care enough to make the sacrificial changes that are needed to secure our economic independence. But even if we are aware and care, nothing will ever be done if we do not *dare* to take a stand! Change always involves risk, and unless we dare to face those risks, we remain on a determined road to financial disaster.

Do we dare to stand up for what is right?

When we asked senators, economists, corporate leaders, and average citizens, "Why don't we pay off the national debt? Why don't we become a debt-free nation? There isn't a down-side risk, is there?" the reactions were predictable. We were answered by raised eyebrows, shocked stares, a few excited reactions, and many negative comments.

Many elected officials don't dare to even dream of paying off the debt because it might mean budget cuts in their own backyards. They often run on the platform of promising what they will do when they are elected. Never are those promises, "I will raise taxes and cut some of your favorite programs so that America can solve its great problem of the national debt." Instead, they promise to spend money on projects requested by powerful, well-organized lobby groups that helped them get elected. This costs the unorganized majority of citizens billions of dollars in taxes. But we are equally guilty when we vote from self-interested positions.

Some politicians do not dare speak out against their party's platform, even if they disagree with it, for fear that they may advance no further or may severely limit their careers within the party. If a senator or representative knows within his or her heart that the party's spending policies or tax policies are wrong, he or she will rarely speak up and openly criticize the party.

Therefore, let us applaud elected officials who have the fortitude to do what they know is right, regardless of what it may do to their political careers. If we can recognize the courage of those individuals who speak out for a platform that limits government spending, gives a lower ceiling to our nation's debt, and demands a balanced budget, then we will take the first step up the mountain of financial freedom.

Do we dare to disagree with the experts who say it can't be done?

Most of us wouldn't dare tackle the debt problem because people who are smarter than we are in the fields of economics and politics tell us it can't be done. They muster facts and figures which are researched and documented to justify their economic theories of why the debt cannot be eliminated.

The most destructive force in an institution or a society is a negative-thinking expert. (An expert is somebody who has more experience or is more knowledgeable in a specific area than the average person.) A negative-thinking expert has had experience and "knows" it won't work. But the truth is, new revelations and discoveries constantly change the scene. A positive-thinking expert is the best person we can find. But a negative-thinking expert is the worst, because nobody dares challenge that individual. Creativity, however, often comes not from the authorities who are entrenched in a field of study, but from an outside observer.

Consider the janitor who was cleaning the front lobby of an old landmark hotel in downtown San Diego. He overheard two well-dressed, professional-looking men talking in the lobby. "We'll just have to cut through the floor above," one of the men said. "And cut through the floor below," the other added. The janitor edged closer to hear better. The two professionals continued to discuss exactly where the holes would be made.

Finally the janitor interrupted, "Pardon me. But it is my job to keep this place clean. What are you talking about?" They introduced themselves as an architect and an engineer, and they were designing a new elevator for the hotel to keep pace with the competition of newer and more modern hotels.

The janitor protested. But you can't cut a hole in the floors from top to bottom, not without closing down the entire hotel!"

"Of course we can," they said. "We've done it before and we'll do it again."

Again the janitor spoke up. "But this hotel is made of plaster walls. If you knock these walls apart, dust is going to go through the hallways and into the rooms, and there's no way I can keep it clean. You'll have to close down the whole operation."

The experts smiled and tried to ignore him. But the janitor was persistent. He looked them straight in the eye and said, "Why don't you just build the elevator on the outside? That way it won't make any mess at all, and everyone will have a nice view of the ocean as they take the ride up!"

From the voice of a janitor came the idea of the first glass elevator on the outside of a hotel, which has since become a trademark of the finest hotels in the world!

Like all other professions, economics is too important to leave to the economists. We will never pay off the debt if we believe we can't do it. And if an economist or politician believes we can't do it, he or she will have facts, figures, and reasons to "prove" why we can't. But attitude is more important than facts.

In a wonderful, readable book, *Conversations with an Economist* (Rowman and Allanheld), Arjo Klamer, professor of economics at Wellesley College, interviewed prominent economists including James Tobin, Karl Brunner, and David Gordon.[4] Professor Klamer found that economists differed widely concerning their theories, and despite volumes of publications and numerous debates, they did not change their minds. The reason, according to Klamer, is that economists develop theories to justify their own political positions.

This is not a criticism of their profession, but an observation of human nature. Facts can always be gathered to support almost any economic viewpoint. Even Nobel-Prize-winning economists differ on the solution to our national debt crisis. Each supports his argument with equal amounts of "undisputed facts." If the economists disagree, how can anyone else dare to believe there is a solution?

Nobel-Prize-winning economist Friedrich A. von Hayek stated that "economists can observe and describe general patterns that emerge in the marketplace, but cannot make precise predictions about the course of the economy." Professor von Hayek said, "Not even a computer can keep track of the daily information that is dispersed among hundreds and thousands of people about their real intention to buy, sell, and invest. They signal them through prices. They often won't say what they intend and don't even know themselves until the moment they find out the price is right"![5]

This is when we must remember that our attitude toward a problem is much more important than any of the facts surrounding it. Consider the amazing feats people have achieved despite the odds and facts against them simply because they believed it was possible. Where a positive attitude pervades, creative solutions abound even in the face of experts who say it can't be done.

Do we dare face the facts?

A wise member of the Crystal Cathedral board of directors, John Joseph, once said, "I am a success because I learned economics from my father."

"What was your father's profession?" I asked.

"He was a lawyer," John answered. When I looked puzzled, he continued, "My dad once told me, 'John, you can't succeed unless you understand basic economics. I'll give it to you in one simple sentence: When your outgo exceeds your income, it's the upstart of your downfall!'"

Today the outgo of the government exceeds its income. Our country's economic condition is comparable to a luxury cruise ship. The orchestra is playing, and the party is in full swing. The sound of laughter fills the ballroom where many couples are dancing. Some passengers have retired early to their staterooms. Unknown to them all is that far beneath the deck of the ship, a hole has been punctured in the hull. Water is slowly leaking in. If the problem is discovered in time, the damage can be limited to the lower levels of the vessel. But if too much time elapses, the results can be devastating. To ignore the danger by listening to the music will lead to certain disaster.

We must dare to face the facts. America has a hole in its budgetary boat. Our outgo exceeds our income. This is the upstart of our downfall!

Do we dare to share the responsibility for the debt?

We must be careful when we criticize our senators and representatives who may vote to increase the debt. We are the ones who put them in office! We must shoulder the responsibility too. We must share in the liability. There can be no rescue until we share in the common goal and take common responsibility for solving this problem. No president can do it alone. No political party can do it alone. They are all powerless without the shared support of an unselfish public.

Do we dare to face the fear of failure? Do we dare to succeed?

Nothing restrains people more than the fear of failure. The major cause of failure is the fear of failure. We are so afraid we will fail that we don't try. When we don't try, our failure is guaranteed instantly and absolutely. Fear of success also keeps some people paralyzed. Whether it is fear of failure or fear of success, we must dare to face our fears to achieve our goals.

America must face the fear of failure as we seek to solve the impossible. Fifty years ago it was impossible to put a man on the moon, transplant a heart, or make a deaf man hear. The idea that we should actually try to pay off the national debt might strike fear of failure in the hearts of our president, elected officials, and top economists.

Do we dare to run the risk of failure? Do we dare to stand up for what is right? Do we dare to disagree with the experts who say it can't be done? Do we dare to share the responsibility for our economic condition? We have no choice but to take this challenge because our national debt is about to engulf us.

The answer to the federal debt is in our attitude. If we are aware, if we are willing to care, and if we have the courage to dare, then a solution is possible. We *can* find the answer!

Provided we practice the power of possibility thinking! What is that . . . ?

4

Possibility Thinkers—
Lead the Way

America is faced with a historical window of opportunity. It is now that we must take up this great challenge to balance the budget, eliminate the mounting yearly deficits, and make a plan to retire the national debt.

To some people this undertaking may seem to be an impossibility. But through the power of possibility thinking, impossibilities can be moved into the realm of the possible.

What precisely is possibility thinking? Possibility thinking is assuming that the ideal can become real. Possibility thinking is sifting carefully through all the alternatives and options, both real and fanciful, in the process of determining the grand objective that should be pursued.

The late Walter Burke was chairman of the board of McDonnell Douglas Corporation in Long Beach, California, when he received a telephone call from President Kennedy. As Walter Burke described it to me, "The president said to me, 'Mr. Burke, I want to put a man on the moon. We both know that's impossible. Now let's figure out a way to make it possible. I'm calling you because we need to have a rocket with enough booster power to push a capsule away from the gravitational pull of the earth. I want you to tackle that part of the total project.'"

It was not much later that Walter Burke called me to

ask if he could have a large photograph of the possibility thinker's creed. The same poster had been distributed to many locker rooms in professional athletic circles. We promptly sent the following poster to Mr. Burke which he kept on the wall behind his desk.

> WHEN FACED WITH A MOUNTAIN
> I WILL NOT QUIT!
> I WILL KEEP ON STRIVING
> UNTIL I CLIMB OVER,
> FIND A PASS THROUGH,
> TUNNEL UNDERNEATH—
> OR SIMPLY STAY
> AND TURN THE MOUNTAIN INTO A GOLD MINE,
> WITH GOD'S HELP!

Possibility thinkers listen to every positive idea. They never reject an idea because there is something wrong with it, because it might release some new tensions, or because it contains an inherent fault or negative factor, actual or implied, within the proposal. Possibility thinkers are smart enough to know there is something wrong with every good idea. Possibility thinkers clearly understand that all great ideas have their own flaws and imperfections. However, possibility thinkers believe that if there is some value or good in the proposal—NO MATTER HOW PREPOSTEROUS AND OFF THE WALL IT MAY SOUND— then the proposal should be taken seriously. It is not a mark of intelligence to scorn, scoff, or snub some way-out idea if, in fact, it does hold some positive potential. History proves that great progress has been made by great dreamers whose ideas at the outset appeared unrealistic, if not ludicrous. Possibility thinkers explore with an imaginative and open mind all of the possibilities in a proposal. Possibility thinkers make an all-out commitment to discover hitherto unknown avenues by which an impossibility could, in time, become a new breakthrough. Strangely enough, this mental attitude alone has the power to release incredible forces that will move an impossible idea into the realm of the possible.

Pay off the entire federal debt? This gives us a fantastic example and opportunity for applied possibility thinking. The almost universal instinctive, intuitive, impulsive reaction is, "But if we can't even balance the budget, how do you expect to pay off the debt?"

It has been observed that when a positive idea comes into the mind, we can almost always expect the positive idea to be immediately followed by a negative thought that can threaten to abort the positive idea at its conception. But every positive idea deserves a fair trial. Just because some splendid dream appears fanciful and unrealistic, if not impossible, doesn't give anybody the right to rudely hiss the idea off center stage or rule it out of court. The greatest ideas are always impossible when first conceived.

If they were well within the realm of possibility and general acceptance, they would not be ideas under discussion—they would be projects already begun. The greatest ideas are those so embryonic that they are unborn and still waiting to be taken seriously.

There is a delightful story of the old fisherman who sat at the end of the pier with his line in the water. At his side was a bucket where he put his catch of the day. Next to the bucket was a ten-inch ruler, stained and splintered. Next to the ruler was a can of worms. A passer-by paused and watched the fisherman's pole bend and saw him enthusiastically land his first fish. He carefully dislodged the hook from the fish's mouth. Holding the squirming fish in one hand, he picked up the ruler with the other to measure the length of his catch. It measured just short of his ten-inch ruler. He seemed pleased and threw the fish into the bucket. The fisherman then hooked another fish, and the pole bent until the tip almost touched the water! As he landed the big one, it was quickly obvious that it was far longer than the ten-inch ruler. He threw this fish back. The passer-by was puzzled, but said nothing. As he watched the old man, he observed that the little fish were put into the bucket to be taken home, but the fish larger than ten inches were thrown back. Curiosity got the better of him, and finally he said to the fisherman, "I'm very curious. Why do you keep the little ones and throw the big ones back?"

"Well," the old fellow answered, "my frying pan is only ten inches wide."

We can laugh at this story, but in reality, who is that fisherman? We are that fisherman. Every person is that fisherman. The truth is, we throw away the biggest ideas that come into our minds. We have our plans, our perceptions, and our prejudices, and if an idea comes along that exceeds or doesn't fit into our plans, we intuitively, instinctively, impulsively—but not necessarily intelligently—discard it out of hand.

The hardest job in the world is to think bigger than we have been thinking before. Thus, the ideas that are bigger than we are able to understand or embrace are offhandedly and irresponsibly discarded.

Intelligent and critical possibility thinkers have learned that ideas are never to be thrown away simply because they are too big for our minds to grasp. We may reserve judgment. We may be cautious before we make a wholehearted commitment. We may quietly hesitate before we plunge ahead. But we discipline ourselves against the natural, normal, negative inclination to simply laugh the idea away and throw the big fish back into the water.

What is true for an individual or for an institution must be true for our country too. We will all rise or fall, succeed or fail, move forward or backward depending upon our willingness to master skills of good management. Management is the control of resources to maximize productivity. Success comes as we establish solid objectives and then manage our resources to achieve the determined goals that have been sensibly established. Institutions, individuals, and nations fail when they fail to manage. Some fail by mismanaging time. Others mismanage money. Still others mismanage people. But ultimately most fail when they mismanage the ideas that flow into their minds.

Possibility thinking is the philosophy that offers universal principles for the effective management of ideas. Ultimately no person, company, organization, or nation suffers from a shortage of money, talent, or time. The problem is always an idea problem. Money flows to dynamic ideas. Talent is attracted to the corporation or the country or the church that has excitement-producing ideas.

In the book *Tough Times Never Last, But Tough People Do!* I listed ten commandments of possibility thinking. These commandments can help us fulfill the dream that the American people could form a national consensus to achieve the objective of becoming a debt-free nation.

This is an idea. We hope it will prove to be an idea whose time has come. But how will this idea be received in the minds of people? How do we manage the thought? How do we respond and react to the proposal? Let us keep in mind the ten commandments for possibility thinking.

Commandment Number One

NEVER REJECT A POSSIBILITY BECAUSE YOU SEE SOMETHING WRONG WITH IT!

There is something wrong with every good idea. No proposal is perfect. There are flaws in every system. It is no mark of intelligence to find something wrong with a great idea. The question is, Is there something good in it? Possibility thinkers assume they can spot the positive and the negative elements in every idea and then proceed to divide the negative from the positive. The negative elements must be isolated and eliminated, or at least insulated or sublimated. Meanwhile, the positive elements in the proposal are extracted, welcomed, nurtured, developed, and exploited with adventure and ultimate success.

Commandment Number Two

NEVER REJECT A POSSIBILITY BECAUSE YOU WON'T GET THE CREDIT!

We would plead with our fellow citizens that the proposal for achieving national financial freedom through the power of being debt free not become a political issue. A tragedy in a free society is the inclination of a cause to become a politicized issue. If Republicans are for it, then Democrats have to be against it. If Democrats advocate it, Republicans had better fight it.

When the bombs fell on Pearl Harbor, there was only one unanimous reaction: we must win the battle and save the country without concern about who gets the credit. The Republicans didn't stop to think, "Well, if we win the war, the democratic president will get the credit." Great things will happen when a company or a community or a country pulls together to win a battle without any concern about who is going to be honored.

God can do tremendous things through the person who doesn't care who gets the credit.

Commandment Number Three

NEVER REJECT AN IDEA BECAUSE IT IS IMPOSSIBLE!

Every great idea is impossible because what makes an idea great is that it is something that isn't being done . . . yet. And it isn't being done because it probably hasn't struck anyone as being a viable venture. I'm convinced that every time a great idea comes from God it is always impossible. The contribution that religion makes to society is the reminder that greatness comes when we walk in the arena of faith. And faith is making a decision before we can see our way through the whole pilgrimage.

Someone said to me recently, "I will be glad to go along with the idea as soon as I can understand it." He elaborated, "I'm willing to become a believer once I get the answers to my questions."

I replied, "But faith is what you need when you can't get answers to the questions!"

Possibility thinkers don't reject an idea because it is impossible, because they can't get answers to their questions, or because they can't see how they are going to accomplish it. They welcome glorious impossibilities as exciting invitations to come up with a new invention, a new organization, or a new technique that could spell triumph anyway.

Commandment Number Four

NEVER REJECT A POSSIBILITY BECAUSE YOUR MIND IS ALREADY MADE UP!

Possibility thinkers recognize that ego, greed, and stubbornness are the three major causes of failure. They are the unholy trinity that block progress. Possibility thinkers do not want their own way; they want to do the right thing. "I'm not ego involved; I'm success oriented," I tell my friends and associates. After all, possibility thinking is pragmatic. I know that if I get my own way—if I'm wrong—I'm going to fail down the line. Then I can suffer a real ego blowout at high speed in heavy traffic!

So, possibility thinkers have the capacity to change their thinking drastically and sometimes swiftly. People who never change their minds are either perfect or stubborn. I don't know of an intelligent person who would claim to be perfect or who would want to be labeled stubborn. Therefore we need never be embarrassed about changing our minds. Rather, it can be a mark of emotional maturity.

Commandment Number Five

NEVER REJECT AN IDEA BECAUSE IT IS ILLEGAL!

Under no circumstances do we permit or advocate or approve of an illegal act. But it is true that much progress is thwarted by regulations, ordinances, and procedures, as well as by county, state, and federal laws. The beautiful thing about a democracy is that we have the power to change laws. And the positive legislators are the persons who are constantly looking for progress-restricting obstacles that exist in society. Then, through legislation, they seek to remove these growth-restricting obstacles. We simply change the laws to allow positive possibilities the opportunity to come alive and bring greater opportunity for all.

Commandment Number Six

NEVER REJECT AN IDEA BECAUSE YOU DON'T HAVE THE MONEY, THE MANPOWER, THE MUSCLE, OR THE MONTHS TO ACHIEVE IT!

The power of a dream outpaces the power of the obstructions. The weight of a positive idea tips the scale when balanced against the weight of the obstacles. In other words, a positive idea has the power to attract the kind of support that can compensate for lack of money, manpower, time, or talent. If a positive possibility is treated with respect and is carefully nurtured, it will succeed against overwhelming odds. Exciting possibilities have a magnetism that attracts the kind of support that can move them from fantasy to reality. Ideas attract money. Ideas attract talent. Ideas solve time problems too. The important thing is *the idea*. Welcome it. Respect it. Trust it. Believe in it.

Commandment Number Seven

NEVER REJECT AN IDEA BECAUSE IT WILL CREATE CONFLICT!

Every new idea will stir some opposition. Every new proposal can offend someone. Every positive possibility has a price tag on it and not everyone will agree upon the price. Every time we set a new goal we will incur some opposition. Every new commitment will produce a new set of conflicts. New tensions arise with every new move forward. Therefore, if we reject an idea because it will create conflict, we will never get anywhere.

Commandment Number Eight

NEVER REJECT AN IDEA BECAUSE IT IS NOT YOUR WAY OF DOING THINGS!

Ultimately your way isn't important. The right way is the only thing that matters. Learn to accommodate. Prepare to compromise. Plan to adjust. A different style, a new policy, a change in tradition are all opportunities to grow. Readjust your budget. Compromise your taste. Accommodate your lifestyle. You may have to decide that it's more important to succeed than it is to snobbishly adhere to your private preferences.

Commandment Number Nine

NEVER REJECT AN IDEA
BECAUSE IT MIGHT FAIL!

Great success comes to the individual or the institution that has the freedom to fail. The *fear* of failure is the number one reason for failure itself just as the possibility of success is the number one explanation for most human achievement. What would you attempt to do today if you knew you could not fail? What goals would you set for yourself if you knew you could succeed? What promises would you make if you knew you could keep them? What dreams would you embrace wholeheartedly and completely if you knew they could come true? This is possibility thinking. It releases incredible energies, enthusiasms, and powers. Ideas that have great possibilities for failure are turned into astonishing accomplishments through the power of possibility thinking!

Commandment Number Ten

NEVER REJECT AN IDEA
BECAUSE IT IS SURE TO SUCCEED!

Does this sound crazy? Ridiculous? Not really. We have seen countless people reject positive ideas because they were afraid of success. "If I succeed, will people expect more from me?" "If I succeed, will I only set higher standards for myself that I'll have to live up to?" "If I succeed, will I be able to handle the success?"

Many companies are deliberately kept small and restrained from expansion by corporate chiefs who fear success. They assume, often correctly, that if the company succeeds they will have to delegate power and authority to others. And to many founding individuals that is a threatening prospect. In the political realm, we all see reactionary politicians voting against great ideas that could possibly succeed and in the process accrue to the advantage of their political opponent.

The ten commandments of possibility thinking help us to manage ideas so effectively that we can be assured of success. Each one has told us what *not* to do. Now let's restate them in positive terms. Possibility thinkers are slow to vote no. They are naturally inclined to vote yes to positive ideas. The yes vote may be qualified: yes, if; yes, when; yes, but; yes, after. But it is always yes. The natural reaction of a possibility thinker is to vote yes to a positive idea.

Commandment Number One

SAY YES TO AN IDEA
IF IT WILL HELP PEOPLE WHO ARE HURTING
NOW OR IN THE FUTURE!

Possibility thinkers recognize that we are all stewards. We are entrusted with a life and are obligated to contribute to the welfare of the human family. An idea is not measured by whether or not it is possible; it is measured by whether or not it is practical. Practicality has nothing to do with the immediate achievement potential within the idea, but rather with the service to humanity that is implied in the proposal. Any time someone comes up with a big, bold, beautiful idea, we do not ask, "Is it possible?" Rather we ask, "Who needs it? Would it help people who are hurting?" The secret of success is to find a need and fill it, find a hurt and heal it, find a problem and solve it, find a chasm and bridge it. If an idea would help people who are hurting, we have no right to vote against it. Our mental attitude must be yes. Perhaps yes, if. Maybe yes, when. Sometimes yes, but. Occasionally yes, after. But never a total, obstinate, arbitrary, concretized no!

Commandment Number Two

SAY YES TO THE IDEA
IF IT CHALLENGES AND MOTIVATES
SELF-DISCIPLINE!

Every person and every institution understands the normal inclination for waste. Expendable resources can too easily be drained away through lack of self-control. Possibility thinking is interested in maximizing productivity. All of us must welcome ideas that, if embraced, would impose the pressures to work harder, save more, and increase the power base to give added strength to the institution, the organization, or the cause that perpetuates the nobler human values.

Commandment Number Three

SAY YES TO AN IDEA
IF IT HOLDS THE PROSPECT OF CONTRIBUTING
TO PEACE, PROSPERITY, AND PRIDE IN THE
HUMAN FAMILY!

In a world marred by wars, poverty, and humiliation in the human family, let there be no offhanded, impulsive rejection of sincere proposals that, however implausible and unrealistic they may seem, do hold some promise of moving the human family closer to prosperity which can eliminate poverty, peace which can eliminate war, and pride which can eliminate human shame.

Commandment Number Four

SAY YES TO AN IDEA
IF IT WILL ENDOW THE GREAT DREAMS OF
GREAT DREAMERS!

History teaches that there are dreamers, there are dreamers, and then there are dreamers! There are the dreamers who have a dream but never pull it off. There are the dreamers who make their dreams come true only to have their dreams die out when they die. Then there are the dreamers who make their dreams come true and inspire their successors to perpetuate their dreams beyond their own lifetimes.

Any idea that will prolong the life span of a great dream of a great dreamer deserves to be taken seriously. There were those great dreamers who dreamed of colleges and watched their dreams come true, only to see those dreams die out for want of a perpetual endowment fund that could capitalize the dream through stormy seasons. The history of private colleges in the United States is littered with shipwrecked dreams of colleges that were founded but were unable to survive the depressions, the wars, and other economic tough times. On the other hand, there are also colleges that were founded with the financial foundation that provided them an unbroken income, enabling them to survive the catastrophic economic earthquakes that history inevitably produces.

If an idea contributes to the endowment of a great dream of a great dreamer, listen to it carefully and take it seriously.

Commandment Number Five

SAY YES TO AN IDEA
IF IT MAKES GOOD FINANCIAL SENSE!

I remember the first time I met W. Clement Stone. At the time he was reputed to be one of the wealthiest men in the United States. "What does it feel like to be superrich?" I asked him.

"It gives me the feeling of power," he answered.

"And what is that feeling of power?" I asked. I'll never forget his answer.

He looked at me and said, "It is a wonderful feeling, if you want to do a lot of good for a lot of people!" And he flashed his wonderful smile.

Great wealth gives you the power to do a lot of good for a lot of people! Any idea that holds the possibility of producing financial advantages for persons or institutions controlled by the nobler human values deserves to be taken seriously.

With its ideals of freedom, peace, and prosperity America should strive to multiply its wealth. The goal of the United States of America should be to become a richer, wealthier nation so that future generations will be empowered to do greater good for the whole world. The poor cannot solve the poverty problem. The hungry cannot solve the famine problem. The enslaved cannot solve the problems of the oppressed. It makes sense for Americans to maximize the wealth that we have today and aim not only at being a debt-free nation, but a nation that will, like a great university, have its own endowment funds. A great president of a great college or university should set as prime objectives not only the establishment of the highest academic credentials but also the building up of an endowment fund to make sure that research and development can be carried out in future generations. That president should strive to build an endowment so that worthwhile students who lack the money to attend the university could be given an opportunity for a free education.

We should call upon the presidents of the United States of America in the coming decades to understand their role to be somewhat like that of the head of a great university. They should establish endowment funds. They should start them and watch them grow. They should build endowment funds in which the capital cannot be touched but the annual earnings can be distributed. I have a dream of a day when the national radio and television networks will converge upon the nation's capital for the announcement of the winners of the scholarships given by the federal government to worthy students. Even as the president of the United States has handed out medals of honor to veterans of wars, and even as the king of Norway has the joy of handing out Nobel Prizes to international achievers, so future presidents of the United States would have the joy of handing out prize scholarship awards from the endowment funds that have yet to be established.

Commandment Number Six

SAY YES TO AN IDEA
IF IT WILL BRING BEAUTY INTO THE WORLD!

Beauty is practical too. Ideas that contribute to color and to cleanliness upgrade the quality of human living and deserve to be taken seriously because human beings are inclined to become more beautiful persons when they live in a more beautiful environment. Environmental ugliness contributes forcefully and forthrightly to moral decline and decadent behavior.

What will happen in American society if the streets are filled with potholes and never repaired, if the paint peels and is never repainted, if windows crack and are not replaced, and if weeds grow through the cracks in the sidewalks and are never removed? We can expect those conditions to exist and to spread like a malignancy throughout the land in the decades to come if our country becomes financially bound by debt. We are one nation, after all. A debt-free America would be a wealthy America. And that would mean the power to ensure the perpetuity of beauty in our cities, in our streets, in our countrysides. We see beautiful parks. We see rolling hills. We see clean streets and clean cities. But it will be in direct proportion to the financial health of our land.

Commandment Number Seven

SAY YES TO AN IDEA IF IT CONTRIBUTES TO A SENSE OF A CARING COMMUNITY!

If an idea has within itself the power or possibility of bringing divergent peoples together into a sense of brotherhood and sisterhood, it has enough value to be looked at honestly.

Many ideas are malicious in their intent. Some individuals and institutions thrive on being divisive. This, after all, is a natural, age-old, reactionary technique of insecure people who elevate themselves by demeaning their real or fanciful competitors.

The truth is that all human beings are living on the same planet, drinking the same water, and breathing the same air. Our earth is a space vehicle traveling at an incredible speed of sixty-seven thousand miles per hour around the sun. And if planet Earth blows up, all nations will blow up together.

There is a beautiful teaching in the Bible that all people are created by God and accountable to Him. That makes us accountable to one another. The world is too dangerous a place today for any nation to be isolationist in its mentality. If one nation suffers, all of us will eventually feel the pain. If water penetrates a boat by entering the most insignificant room of the vessel, it will be only a matter of time before the captain in his luxurious quarters will be affected too.

We must recognize the truth in the phrase that no man is an island. No nation can stand alone. We must constantly keep before us a vision of a world that is a united collection of human beings. And the universality of the human family's needs must transcend our individual selfish goals. If an idea will contribute to the possibility of happiness and health for all nations, then of course it must be taken seriously, however grandiose it may appear. We will not say no to any idea that holds within itself the prospect of a world of brotherhood and sisterhood of human beings. We may qualify our yes if, yes but, yes after, or yes when, but we will not say no. We have a dream of an America that is so financially powerful, a country with all its debts paid, a mature institution well endowed with cash surpluses, that it will have the power and clout to produce peace and prosperity for our whole world!

Commandment Number Eight

SAY YES TO AN IDEA
IF IT WILL CONTRIBUTE TO THE COLLECTIVE
SELF-ESTEEM
OF A PERSON OR A NATION!

Self-esteem and possibility thinking are philosophical Siamese twins. The "I am" always determines the "I can." The individual or institution that has a strong self-image will dream noble dreams. The individual or institution that suffers from an inferiority complex will never dare to dream what it can do, what it can be, or what it can accomplish. More than anything else an individual's self-image will contribute to the quality of the visions the mind creates.

All of the wealth and all of the power, without genuine, healthy pride, are nothing. For nearly one hundred years now a new "science" called psychiatry has tried to arrive at the ultimate motivation that makes a human being a person. Dr. Viktor Frankl, lecturing at Claremont Theological Seminary in Claremont, California, said that to Sigmund Freud the ultimate human motivation was will to pleasure. Freud thought the single, strongest need within the human being was the need for pleasure drives to be fulfilled. Alfred Adler, said Frankl, thought the ultimate human motivation was not will to pleasure, but will to power. Adler thought humans were primarily motivated by lust for power. Frankl himself, however, thought the ultimate human motivation was the will to meaning. He said that more than anything else, people need to see that there is some meaning, some value, some purpose to what is going on.

I thought about that lecture for many years. It directed me down avenues of study in books and in conferences. Years later in a three-hour private dialogue with the esteemed Dr. Frankl, I shared my position: "Dr. Frankl, I submit that deeper than the will to pleasure, deeper than the will to power, deeper than the will to meaning is the *will to dignity*."

Even meaning loses meaning unless and until it feeds my need for self-esteem and human dignity. We now know from behavioral sciences that the lack of self-esteem is the single most important cause of almost every negative human behavior imaginable. Any idea, therefore, that contributes to a personal or collective sense of self-esteem ought to seriously attract our vote and our support.

The goal of a debt-free America holds the prospect of building a nation that will enjoy a patriotic self-esteem at the highest level of any nation in the history of the human race. Psychologists have long known that people with a strong sense of self-esteem tend to be open, generous, and nondefensive. Therefore they are easy and wonderful to live with. That's the kind of America that the world would welcome! On the other hand, insecure people and insecure nations, suffering from inferiority complexes or a lack of noble pride, are defensive, selfish, and basically dangerous.

Commandment Number Nine

SAY YES TO AN IDEA
IF IT IS A POSITIVE SOLUTION
TO A NEGATIVE CONDITION!

Possibility thinkers are aware of the fact that there is a positive and a negative solution to every problem.

The challenge of morality is to accept the restraints of law that would protect us from the temptation to select the negative solutions to human problems. For instance, the Ten Commandments in the Old Testament given by God to Moses were not designed to keep human beings from enjoying life. They were given to protect us from the negative solutions to human pressures and problems. Reckless antisocial behavior will ultimately rob us of the joy of living. For instance, people who kill can expect to be killed. Men who commit adultery can expect to have a fight with a husband of a philandering wife. People who lie can expect to lose the confidence and trust of fellow human beings. Moral restraints protect us from the inclination to accept negative solutions to problems. To get out of a problem by lying is the negative approach. We welcome, then, solutions to problems that are within the restraints of moral law and that would protect us from taking the cheap and easy way out of a predicament.

The vast majority of religious people have always opposed abortion. Why? Because they view abortion as a negative solution to a problem. The positive solution would be to allow a unique creature, a one-of-a-kind individual, to come into human existence and have his or her chance to contribute to society. Ideas that restrict our moral freedoms are not to be viewed as violations of our liberty but are to be seen primarily as screens that can protect us from the temptation to accept negative solutions.

The elimination of our federal debt is a moral issue. The alternative is to continue to increase the debt for our personal self-indulgences today and pass on the expense of servicing that liability to unborn generations. That is a form of taxation without representation. It is theft!

Commandment Number Ten

**SAY YES TO AN IDEA
IF IT CHALLENGES US TO THINK BIGGER
AND HAVE MORE FAITH!**

Any idea that would help the human family and at the same time would appear to be impossible is to be welcomed as a challenge to our belief system. In 1967 the World Psychiatric Congress was held in Madrid, Spain. The closing session dealt with the subject "Human Values of Psychotherapy." The first lecturer dealt with the human value of faith. The second lecturer dealt with the human value of hope. The third lecturer dealt with the human value of love. More than four thousand delegates at the convention, including me, heard the challenge to welcome opportunities that would build faith, inspire hope, or generate love. These qualities mark emotionally and mentally healthy persons.

The same can apply to a nation. How can we build faith? Any great idea that appears to be impossible holds the fabulous potential of becoming a faith-building experience. Individuals and institutions are only as strong as their inner confidence and belief systems. Ultimately this inner spirit of dynamic faith cannot be inherited, nor can it be institutionalized effectively in a Declaration of Independence, a Bill of Rights, or a national Constitution. Ultimately it must be discovered by each new generation. Each new generation must face its own mountain and move it! Each new generation must confront its own wars and win them! Each new generation must tackle its own impossible challenge and overcome it! This continuous process of discovery, rediscovery, and renewal of belief and faith is made possible as new ideas come to challenge us to move some glorious impossibility into the realm of the possible.

Possibility thinkers, let's unite! Let's tackle the great idea of creating a debt-free America for the glory of God and for the peace, the prosperity, and the pride of all human beings on planet earth.

5

The Power of Being Debt Free

We Americans have a history of producing innovative solutions to unsolvable problems, of creating new ideas for new tomorrows. In the 1940s scientists were certain that an airplane could not travel faster than the speed of sound. But a group of United States Air Force pilots believed it was possible, and in 1947 Captain Charles Yeager broke the sound barrier. Since then, airplanes have traveled in excess of five times the speed of sound.

In a Los Angeles ear clinic, totally deaf children and adults are being made to hear for the first time in their lives. Through an ingenious electronic implant in the inner ear, microscopic hair follicles are stimulated to transfer the vibrations of sound into nerve impulses, successfully restoring the sensation of sound to hundreds of deaf people.

In the Midwest, the first lithotripter, a kidney stone crusher, has been developed to treat patients with shock waves in order to dissolve kidney stones without the usual painful surgery and prolonged recovery time.

In all fields of life, human beings have solved unsolvable problems or created new and innovative methods of dealing with their problems. The imagination of the human being constantly amazes us with the wonderful products and services being created.

If we can break the sound barrier, make the deaf hear, and develop machines to heal our hurts, isn't it possible that we can creatively solve the problem of the federal debt? Or is this a bit crazy? Is it too idealistic? Who will really make the world a better place, the realist or the idealist? The dreamer or the cynic? No dreamer is ever crazy because the dreamer becomes the uplifting force that gives people and institutions a vision. Without dreams and visions, we will die!

The Man of La Mancha is a musical play based on the Spanish classic *Don Quixote*. The dreamer Don Quixote sees windmills as evil knights, his decrepit horse as a noble steed, and an ugly cleaning lady in an inn, who is also an abused prostitute, as a beautiful and high-bred maiden. The beautiful part of the story is that those who listen to him become more like Don Quixote's dreams. He gives them self-esteem.

When confronted by the cold, calculating cynics for being a wild dreamer, Don Quixote responds, "Who's crazy? Am I crazy because I see the world as it could become? Or is the world crazy because it sees itself as it is?"

The dream of a debt-free society through possibility thinking is the hope our future generations have for a fiscally stable society. Unless as a nation we are motivated to believe that our economic freedom is possible, then we will give in to the crippling forces of our rising federal debt.

The solution does not lie in intricate details of economic theory. The key is not found by finely tuning government policies. The answer centers on motivating all Americans. The solution is within each one of us.

Recently we had a delightful interview with Arthur Laffer, one of our country's leading economists. As we sat down to breakfast, he immediately offered us a copy of the book *Foundations of Supply-Side Economics* which he wrote with Victor Canto and Douglas Joines. We opened it to one of the middle pages and it appeared to be in a foreign language. We couldn't understand any of it.

We attempted polite smiles, showing that we appreciated his gift, and hoping to communicate that we were dying to go home and read it. But Dr. Laffer anticipated our thoughts. "Have you ever tried teaching a lot of students?" he asked. "Especially teaching them the stuff in that book? They sit there thinking, 'Oh, I should never have come to this class.' What do you do to keep their attention? You have to provide incentives, motivation. In fact, economics is the study of motivation."

His words shocked us. He made us realize that it is time for our nation to make a major shift in its economic thinking. *We must change from mathematical economics to motivational economics.* Possibility thinking must play a major role in developing an attitude that leads to finding solutions to our national debt crisis.

There will be people who will read this and think, *How simple. How shallow. I must have a more intricate plan, one full of numbers and projections in order to convince me that we should take the first step toward eliminating the national debt.*

But we were encouraged by Dr. Laffer who said, "There's an old motto: 'Just because it's simple doesn't mean it's wrong.' I would rather be approximately correct than precisely wrong. And even the top economists can be precisely wrong. The spirit of what you are saying—far more than the exact recipe—strikes me as being right."

Dr. Laffer went on to say, "I was the chief economist for two years with George Shultz. And any time I had a debate with David Stockman or an economist in front of the president, we would get into talking about tiny, detailed numbers. But they have nothing to do with the truth. Because of the immensity of the federal budget, no human being can handle a discussion of those tiny numbers. They

In general, V may rise more or less than R when the wage rate rise. We assume, however, that the tax rates are low enough and workers get a high enough share of the benefits from government spending so that

$$V_w > R_w \qquad (25)$$

In that case, individual n chooses to work if the wage rate exceeds w^*, for then $V > R$; and he chooses not to work if the wage rate falls short of w^*, for then $V < R$. Define w^* to be zero if $\lim_{w \to 0}(V - R) > 0$ and to be infinite if $\lim_{w \to \infty}(V - R) < 0$. It then follows that

$$w^* = W(\tau_1, \ldots, \tau_m; \gamma_1, \ldots, \gamma_m; k_1, \ldots, k_m; n) \qquad (26)$$

is a well-defined function if the τ_is are not too large and if the k_is are not too small.

Equation (22) implies that

$$W_{\tau_i} = \frac{(R_{\tau_i} - V_{\tau_i})}{(V_w - R_w)}, \qquad i = 1, \ldots, m \qquad (27)$$

$$W_{\gamma_i} = \frac{(R_{\gamma_i} - k_i V_{\gamma_i k_i})}{(V_w - R_w)}, \qquad i = 1, \ldots, m \qquad (28)$$

$$W_{k_i} = \frac{(R_{k_i} - \gamma_i V_{\gamma_i k_i})}{(V_w - R_w)}, \qquad i = 1, \ldots, m \qquad (29)$$

and

$$W_n = \frac{-V_n}{(V_w - R_w)} \qquad (30)$$

It is straightforward to use Eqs. (20), (21), (2) and (8)–(13) to show that

$$V_{\tau_i} = \frac{U_c\{-w^2 U_c \sum \gamma_i k_i \tau_i + (1 - \gamma_i k_i)[(1 - \tau)^2 w^2 U_{cc} + 2(1 - \tau)w U_{ch} + U_{hh}]\}}{D}$$

$$< 0, \qquad i = 1, \ldots, m \qquad (31)$$

$$V_{\gamma_i k_i} = -\frac{\tau_i w h U_c[(1 - \tau)^2 w^2 U_{cc} + 2(1 - \tau)w U_{ch} + U_{hh}]}{D}$$

$$> 0, \qquad i = 1, \ldots, m \qquad (32)$$

$$V_n = -f'(n) < 0 \qquad (33)$$

$$R_{\tau_i} = U_c[w H_{\tau_i} \sum (1 - k_i)\gamma_i \tau_i + w H(1 - k_i)\gamma_i] \gtrless 0, \qquad i = 1, \ldots, m \quad (34)$$

$$R_{\gamma_i} = U_c[k_i w H_{\gamma_i k_i} \sum (1 - k_i)\gamma_i \tau_i + (1 - k_i)\tau_i w H] \gtrless 0, \qquad i = 1, \ldots, m \qquad (35)$$

and

$$R_{k_i} = U_c[w \gamma_i H_{\gamma_i k_i} \sum (1 - k_i)\gamma_i \tau_i - \gamma_i k_i w H] < 0, \qquad i = , \ldots, m \qquad (36)$$

will kill any effort to look at the real problem. The simple answer is the right answer. We need to get back to basic principles that even a congressman can understand. Then you'll be able to answer the problem!"

We spoke with other economists, and they also gave us their encouraging support. Martin Feldstein, former chairman of the president's Council of Economic Advisors and economics professor at Harvard University; Gary Shilling, president of Shilling and Company, an economics consulting firm; John Templeton, founder of the Templeton Fund and one of the leading investment analysts in the world; and J. Peter Grace, chief executive officer of W. R. Grace Company all agreed with the spirit of our desire to motivate the American public to get involved in our economic process. Most of them felt that we had a greater chance to bring the importance of this issue to the American people than they did as "experts." Their responses reaffirmed the universal principle that economics is too important to leave to the economists, theology is too important to leave to the theologians, and architecture is too important to leave to the architects!

Not only did we interview economists and business leaders, but we questioned every United States senator and member of the House of Representatives, asking them their opinion on the budget deficit and the reasons for the underlying debt our nation has accumulated. We asked them if they agreed or disagreed with the following statements:

> The federal debt never needs to be repaid. We simply refinance it, generation after generation, and continue to pay interest on that debt as part of the federal budget.

> A plan should evolve and a decision be made to repay the entire federal debt with the goal of becoming a nation that does not have to spend part of its budget to pay the interest on debts.

We received more than 250 responses, and only three agreed with the first statement. The rest shared our concern that we must plan now to deal with the debt in our lifetime. Many senators and representatives not only answered the brief questionnaire but also responded with lengthy letters and reports on their own efforts to creatively eliminate the budget deficit and reduce the federal debt. They were reacting to the many letters they had received from voters in their districts and states. They were eager to share their view with us and support us in the movement to balance the budget and pay off the debt. Here are a few of their comments:

> It will take Congress and the Administration working together to reduce this major problem.
> Congressman Nick J. Rahall, II (D, W. Va.)

> I believe that we in Congress should treat our national fiscal integrity the same way we treat our personal finances—by keeping them healthy and current.
> Congressman Robert E. Badham (R, Calif.)

> This plan to repay the debt will require the unified and long-term commitment on behalf of both the Congress and the people. In so doing, our posterity will not be shouldered with the ever-increasing and unmanageable burden of interest payments on the national debt.
> Congressman James V. Hansen (R, Utah)

> Agreement [that the debt never needs to be repaid] would mean that ultimately we mortgage away any future for our children and grandchildren.
> Congressman Daniel R. Coats (R, Ind.)

> Realistically, the first order of business must be to balance the Federal budget and keep outlays from exceeding receipts. Toward that end, I am the principal author of the Balanced Budget Constitutional Amendment passed by the Senate in the 97th Congress. Once the budget is brought into balance, I would hope we could

go a step further and begin to pay off the national debt.
Senator Strom Thurmond (R, S.C.)

[Let's] retire the public debt once and for all.
Congressman Glenn M. Anderson (D, Calif.)

While this country is currently enjoying a strong and
vibrant economic recovery, the deficit is often an un-
popular topic of discussion. Although most legislators
would agree that it must be addressed, there is currently no real impetus for the adoption of effective and
permanent action. It is inconceivable to me that this
country can simply roll over the deficit and continue to
function. In my mind, that is simply not an alternative.
We must make the difficult but necessary decisions to
turn around this trend towards economic disaster.
Senator Paula Hawkins (R, Fla.)

I feel strongly that some mechanism must be initiated
to not only wipe out the deficit, but to pay off the national debt as well. This cannot be accomplished in-
stantaneously, but a long-range program is mandatory.

In a person's everyday life, one cannot continue to live
on borrowed money. There is always a day of reckoning. This is also true with our Federal Government.
Congressman James H. Quillen (R, Tenn.)

We must continue to push for an Amendment to the
Constitution to balance the federal budget. If Congress
will not cut spending voluntarily, it must be forced to.
Congressman Dan Burton (R, Ind.)

Of all the challenges our nation faces at home and
abroad, none is more important than reducing the unacceptably high level of deficits that threatens our
economy and that of the world. We need less par-
tisanship, more statesmanship. And we need representatives who care more about the next generation and
less about the next election.
Congressman Don Sundquist (R, Tenn.)

Although the senators and representatives differed in
their views on how the deficits and debt should be financed,

they all agreed that somehow it should be done. With additional pressure from the public, our elected officials can put aside their differences and devise a plan to once and for all eliminate federal deficits and repay our national debt. There is no substitute for a determined public, Congress, and administration who will muster the political will to resolve this problem. All Americans must put aside self-interest for our national interest and our children's secure future.

The solution to our economic challenge, the way to stop the theft of our children's financial future, is to be found in two words: *attitude and commitment.* As a nation, we need a positive attitude that arises from a firm belief that we can succeed, and we need a strong commitment to accomplish the goal no matter what the cost. That commitment should be the result of a careful decision. If we have an open, creative, positive attitude as we seek ways to pay off the debt and if we make a solid commitment to pay it off before we know how to solve all of the problems, then we will have taken the most important step.

Attitude

Consider the difference an attitude makes within a financially troubled company. Within the last five years, two corporate giants—the Manville Corporation and Chrysler Corporation—both faced financial problems that would make even the most optimistic financial consultant cringe. Today, one company has been declared insolvent; the other has risen to reclaim its rightful place among the leading corporations of America. What made the difference? It wasn't the rescue loans. It wasn't the quality of the product. It wasn't the cooperation of the unions. All of those factors were important to Chrysler, but the real difference was a positive attitude.

In August 1982, the directors of the Manville Corporation sat around their boardroom table discussing their corporate problems and bleak future. The billion-dollar forest products and construction company was faced with 16,500 lawsuits as a result of its role in producing asbestos-related products. Although the corporation was financially sound and had a low debt-to-equity ratio, it filed for bankruptcy because of the potential loss from the lawsuits. The directors had decided their problems were unsolvable. Why should they drag out the inevitable? Why not just declare bankruptcy? Throw in the towel. Let's quit!

The *Wall Street Journal* reported that the move was "highly unusual and unexpected."[1] The stockholders' equity plummeted from a high of $26.50 per share to nothing. The corporate leaders had lost control, and the company and all the investors had lost their money and faith.

In another part of America several years earlier, the directors of the Chrysler Corporation met to discuss their financial problems. The country was in a deep recession. Auto sales had fallen off dramatically. The company was billions of dollars in debt. In 1980, it lost $1.7 billion, the largest operating loss in United States corporate history. The future looked bleak. If any company should give up, it should have been Chrysler. But after hours of deliberation, a decision was made: we will not quit! There will be a way. We don't know what it is, but we will find it. We are willing to make changes. We are willing to listen.

Over the next months, the unions agreed to unprecedented "givebacks." Twenty thousand white-collar jobs were eliminated as overhead was cut. The federal government made loan guarantees of $1.2 billion (on which it has earned an estimated $800 million in interest and fees). The engineers designed new and better products. The number of different parts needed fell from fifty-three thousand in 1981 to less than forty thousand in 1984. Chrysler's directors had a positive attitude that arose from a firm belief that they would succeed in their goal of putting their corporation back on its feet as a leading automaker in America.

By August 1982—the same month Manville declared bankruptcy—Chrysler had paid off all of its government-backed debts. It re-employed and offered job security to thousands of union members. It designed a new and exciting line of products, including minivans and the reborn convertible! Chrysler stock soared from two dollars to thirty-six dollars a share. Its investors made money and gained renewed confidence in the company. Its challenging slogan became known nationwide: If you can find a better built car, buy it! Chrysler's corporate chief, Lee Iacocca, has been acclaimed by several polls as one of the most respected corporate leaders in America.

What was the difference between Chrysler's success and Manville's bankruptcy? Attitude! There were many important factors along Chrysler's comeback road, but the most important element, the impulse that pushed the company to the top, was the decision not to quit but to win and succeed. The directors realized they didn't have a money problem, they just had an idea problem.

The effect of the attitude factor goes beyond the financial boardrooms of America. It can also make the difference in a country's survival as a sound financial entity.

In the late 1970s, the country of Turkey was the world's most experienced "down and outer." Now it has become a shining example that international bankers point to when they say there is hope for countries that are unbelievably burdened by debt. The head of the International Monetary Fund, Jacques de Larosière, points out that Turkey took a bold step to make the necessary changes to pay off its national and foreign debt. The Organization of Economic Development has said that Turkey's successes are far-reaching and courageous. The World Bank has called Turkey's restructuring program one of the most significant undertaken by a developing country in recent history.

At the peak of its debt crisis, Turkey owed billions of dollars. Inflation was more than 107 percent yearly. Exports were virtually flat. Interest rates were rising. But Turkey made a decision, a decision to pay off its foreign loans and indebtedness. The country's leaders asked for support from the people of Turkey. The people decided they should vote for their grandchildren, not for themselves. Both peasants and businessmen made sacrifices. It wasn't easy, but the people had a new attitude. A poor farmer resigned to earning less said, "Of course, Turkey owes money. Every one of us knows that." The Turks hardly complained. Rather, they stood behind their government's new policies in hopes that it would make a difference.

It did. Annual inflation dropped from 107 percent to 37 percent; exports rose to 11 percent of GNP; the debt fell to $16 billion. And during a world recession, Turkey's economy grew at a pace of more than 4 percent. In the fall of 1984, the Turkish government took another bold step by preparing to sell hundreds of state-owned companies to private investors. As many as 263 enterprises, including Turkish airlines, Turkish Petroleum Company, and the National Post, Telegraph, and Telephone Administration, were expected to be offered for sale at the new Istanbul Securities Exchange. The *Wall Street Journal* called the move Turkey's "most daring gamble yet to spur a free market economy."[2] Although Turkey has a long way to go, the attitude of its citizens is making a difference!

Commitment

A positive attitude that arises from a firm belief that one can succeed is essential. But action is also necessary. There needs to be a strong commitment to accomplish a goal no matter what the cost.

The famous scientist Renè DuBos once said in effect that the human being has a natural and overwhelming inclination to adjust downward. It was one of the reasons why he could be tempted to be a cynic and pessimist.

Adjustment is always a downward movement. Upward movement is never an adjustment; it is always a commitment. Chrysler made a commitment. Turkey made a commitment. Any great company or country that has faced financial disaster and pulled out of it did so because of a commitment.

To not make a commitment is to commit to do nothing. Without a commitment, the natural adjustment downward will begin to take control. It is time for the American people to stop accepting the downward pressures that could lead to financial ruin. We need to make a commitment to move forward and upward again to become a stronger, more financially secure country.

I personally experienced this commitment-making process and the outcome when our church was in the process of building our new sanctuary, the Crystal Cathedral. Architect Philip Johnson delivered a six-inch plastic model of what is today an all-glass church 414 feet long and 126 feet high. I took one look at it and said, "Wow! That has to be built! How much will it cost?"

Philip Johnson answered, "About $7 million."

I quickly calculated in my mind what that would cost if it were mortgaged at the then current interest rate. To borrow $7 million at 9 percent interest, our annual interest payment would be approximately $630,000 the first year! And our total church income was only $2 million. I could not envision how we could have a capital funds drive that would bring in an additional $630,000 a year. We simply did not have that kind of financial base.

The project was financially impossible. But I could not accept the word *impossible*. I also could not think of borrowing that much money and increasing our indebtedness. It was a totally impossible dream from a financial perspective, unless I could make a radical, revolutionary, 360-degree turn in my thinking, namely, to pay cash and dedicate the building debt free. But that brought out a contradiction: If we couldn't make a $630,000 annual payment, how could we possibly raise $7 million?

Desperate, I decided to play the possibility thinking game. I started to write down ten ways to do what I knew was impossible. When you do this, you will be surprised how your attitude will change from "it's impossible" to "it might be possible." I wrote down ways we could pay cash for the building:

> 1. Find 1 person who could donate $7,000,000. (That was good for a laugh, which at least relaxed me to keep going.)
> 2. Find 7 people who could donate $1,000,000 each.
> 3. Find 14 people who could donate $500,000 each.
> 4. Find 28 people who could donate $250,000 each.
> 5. Find 70 people who could donate $100,000 each.
> 6. Find 100 people who cold donate $70,000 each.
> 7. Find 140 people who could donate $50,000 each.
> 8. Find 280 people who could donate $25,000 each.
> 9. Sell all 10,866 windows in the Cathedral for $500 each. (That would raise more than $5 million.)

That was as far as I got. I was already enthusiastic. I believed that the project was possible when only minutes before I believed it was a total impossibility. Creativity happens when you are released from anxieties and tensions. As I relaxed and had fun dreaming up ways to pay for the cathedral, I was able to break out of my negative-thinking predicament.

I knew I had to get one $1 million kickoff gift to lead the enthusiasm for this project. But I didn't know anyone that rich. I remembered reading about a local businessman who had given a $1 million gift to the YMCA. I didn't know him, but I contacted him. When I arrived at his home and showed him the model of the Crystal Cathedral, he whistled with excitement.

"What will you need to get it going?" he asked.

"A leadoff gift of $1 million. That would show everyone that this is something big that is going to happen. Then people will take it seriously. I'd like you to give that $1 million."

Suddenly he lost his enthusiasm. "Well," he stammered, "I would like to, but I can't."

"O.K.," I said. "I'd like to close our visit with prayer." And with that I prayed, "Thank You, God, that John wants to give $1 million. But he says he can't. Please make it possible for him to give it."

I left his house never expecting to see him again. The next morning I received a phone call from him. "Reverend," he said, "it is not a question of *if*. It is a question of *how* and *when*."

I almost fainted with ecstasy. He continued, "That building has to be built. I'll give you a million dollars, but I cannot tell you how or when I'll give it."

Within sixty days he delivered fifty-five thousand shares of his company's stock valued at over eighteen dollars a share. Suddenly the $7 million building looked feasible. But then we decided to build a complete basement, which immediately increased the cost by 50 percent. So we launched a donation campaign to "sell" 10,866 windows at five hundred dollars each. The response was fantastic. It looked as if we could pay cash for the building after all.

Then the unexpected happened. Double-digit inflation hit the marketplace. In just twelve months our project was no longer costing $10 million but $13 million. One year later, when we were into the planning twenty-four months of the program, the cost had increased by another $3 million. We were up to $16 million. Suddenly, before we knew it, the cathedral was going to cost $20 million!

What could we do? I knew what I would do. I took a break. I was on vacation when the church board met to consider an unexpected commercial loan offer for $10 million.

It would allow us to proceed without the enormous strain of fund raising. I returned home to find that the board had accepted the loan.

I was not enthusiastic. How could we pay the interest on $10 million? And the loan was to be tied to the prime rate! Neither I nor a single member of that church board could foresee that by the time the cathedral was completed, the prime rate would be 20 percent!

All I knew was that once we accepted the loan, the pressure would be off my back to try to solicit major gifts from people I hadn't even met yet. Getting a loan has a way of making a person feel as if the job is done! In fact, it is only a big show. You've only deferred the payment.

I was still consumed by my grandest dream: pay for the building and dedicate it debt free. Then when the dedication ceremony was over, I wouldn't be left with the horrendous job of balancing the budget year after year. I made a personal decision not to finish the building unless it could be totally underwritten by cash gifts or cash pledges.

It meant crisscrossing the country building new friendships, selling the cathedral idea, and soliciting funds to get it built. I kept remembering the saying, "Whatever the mind can conceive, the human being can achieve."

On September 18, 1980, the Crystal Cathedral opened its doors. It was an international press event noted and photographed in major media publications around the world. But the only thing that impressed me was that God had answered our prayers.

The cost topped $20 million. We had collected just under $17 million. Four million dollars had been pledged to be given over the next thirty-six months. That was covered by a 9 percent fixed-rate mortgage by our local bank. We announced that the building was dedicated debt free, and in fact, all of the pledges were made good in the next three years.

I felt free! Feelings of "isn't it great not to have a debt" flooded over me. I thought, *Isn't it wonderful not to have to take money out of the offering plate to pay the interest on the mortgage? All the money can go to programs that meet human needs here and now.*

There is nothing like the power of being debt free. It is time for our country to experience that feeling. It is time for our elected officials to know the feeling of not owing $1.836 trillion and not having to raise over $114 billion for an interest payment. It is time to stop stealing from our children. If America were debt free, all of our money could go to programs to meet human needs here and now.

A Movement

Our country can experience this power. It all starts with an attitude. Then it takes a commitment. With a total commitment made by the entire American public to do their part to pay off the federal debt, it is possible to do it. When people unite to solve a problem, anything is possible. When movements mount, mountains move!

We are calling for a movement of the American people to come up with creative, innovative, possibility-thinking, problem-solving solutions. Top economists and corporate leaders, secretaries and salesmen, educators and businessmen—if everyone in America will join this movement, we will come up with an avalanche of ideas to creatively solve the problem of the federal debt.

The solution is in our attitude. There is no hopeless situation until we become hopeless people. Great ideas to solve our national debt will come from ordinary people, for great people are ordinary people with an extraordinary amount of determination.

Already an underground movement to reduce the national debt is appearing throughout the United States across a wide spectrum of people, from the very wealthy to retired individuals who live on nothing more than social security pensions. A recent newspaper article revealed some of the power of this movement. The headline read, "Citizens Chip Away at National Debt."

> WASHINGTON—Deep in the caverns of the U.S. Treasury, little pieces of change are dropping into that bottomless bucket known as the national debt.
>
> As Congress battles over the $1.5 trillion obligation and politicians argue over who is reducing what and when, people all across America are taking matters into their own hands and quietly writing checks.
>
> They have been doing it for years. Since 1961 a little over $1 million has been sent in by people of all ages and occupations who find they have a few extra bucks and figure Uncle Sam needs it more than they do.
>
> They send in a dollar here or five there, or $100 or several thousand to the little-known Public Debt Reduction Fund in the Bureau of Government Financial Operations in the U.S. Treasury.
>
> The fund was established after Texas multimillionaire Sarah Vaughn Clayton died and willed $20 million of her estate to the federal government so it could get a handle on deficit spending.
>
> It didn't.
>
> But that has not discouraged thousands of private citizens from passing the word and the hat over the last 23 years and doggedly tossing those drops into that bucket.
>
> A retired military man writes to say the Army gave him an extra $200 when he was discharged and he wants to give it back.
>
> An elderly man sends in a card that says "Happy Birthday America" every year since 1976 and encloses a check equal to his age. His last check was for $83.

In New Berlin, Wisconsin, Kay Fishburn has orga-
nized something called the Debt Retirement Network
and mails letters around the country asking people to
pitch in.

In Washington, D.C., Lloyd Temem runs a one-man
American Way Committee to Retire the National Debt
because he feels that "more and more people are real-
izing they can make a difference."

And out in Hollywood of all places, movie producer
John Romain has pledged that at least one-fourth of the
ticket sales on his new film—"Still Life with Wood-
pecker," based on a novel by Tom Robbins—will go to
the Treasury.

"A lot of people have been feeling so helpless for so
long," said Romain. "The national debt seems impossible and nobody can afford to do anything about it
alone. But together maybe we can get something rolling."[3]

(Reprinted courtesy of the *Boston Globe*.)

But the movement does not stop there. In Washington,
D.C., a group known as The National Taxpayers Union
monitors government spending and lobbies to control government waste. It has successfully pressured Congress into
saving millions of dollars.

In the September 10, 1984, *Wall Street Journal* a full
page ad, sponsored by the Bipartisan Budget Coalition,
called for a common commitment to cut the deficit. The
coalition includes four former United States secretaries of
the Treasury, the very people who have affixed their signatures to the circulated paper currency in the United
States. Its list of members ranges from The United States
League of Savings Institutions and The National Small
Business Association to The Retail Floorcovering Institute,
the Brick Institute of America, and the American Bus Association.

A grassroots movement all across America is starting

to grow. An aware, aroused, impassioned constituency can make a difference. Members of the public are not powerless. We have voices. We can vote. And our representatives in Congress are listening. There will be change if the American people demand it! Already much of congressional debate centers around the budget deficit issue. There is pressure on representatives, senators, and all elected officials to do something to balance our budget.

6

★

Ten Ways to Accomplish the Impossible—Part One

A debt-free America is a big, bold, beautiful dream! The fulfillment of this dream will require the unrestrained commitment of courageous Americans wholeheartedly dedicated to producing creative solutions and willing to pay the price to carry them out. We believe Americans understand the severity of our country's debt crisis and are willing to make the necessary commitment to do something about it.

During the months of research for this book, we asked economists, corporate leaders, senators, representatives, former presidents, relatives, waiters, secretaries, flight attendants, ministers, and anyone else who would give us the time what they thought of our dream of a debt-free America. Almost everyone agreed that, yes, it would be a wonderful idea, but almost everyone qualified that *yes*.

- Yes, if we do so without surrendering our position in the international marketplace.
- Yes, but not at the sacrifice of medical and social programs that insure the well-being of the underprivileged.
- Yes, but not at the expense of the collapse of our highways and infrastructures.
- Yes, but not at the price of eliminating research that can lead to incredible medical advances.

- Yes, when the nation can provide financial security out of its surplus rather than from its deficits financed by government notes and bonds.
- Yes, but how? How do you accomplish the impossible?

We have often proposed that an impossible situation moves close to the realm of possibility once we begin to play the possibility thinking game, which is an exercise in creative thinking, a variation of brainstorming. In the final analysis, all problems are the same, whether they are intensely personal and apparently small problems, or whether they are urgent national problems of massive proportions. Essentially the problems are the same: challenges to creative thinking. That's all they are. Problems are pressures to be more productive and inventive in our thinking. As we have said, "No person has a money problem, only an idea problem!"

I have seen small problems as well as enormous problems solved by playing the possibility thinking game. The technique is amazingly simple. Take a sheet of paper, write down the numbers one to ten, then force yourself to come up with ten solutions to what you have accepted in your mind as an unsolvable problem. Inevitably, in the process you will come up with enough possibilities to give you, at the very least, a sense of hope.

Be mentally open to any wonderful, wild, eyebrow-raising, even preposterous solution to your problem that may come into your mind. You can expect to break out laughing more than once, for some of the wackiest ideas will quite understandably develop from what has now become your truly liberated imagination. The point is that creativity happens in an environment of relaxation. The tranquil mind is receptive to genuinely creative ideas that form the seeds for real breakthroughs. Humor naturally relaxes a person, which sets the stage for creativity. Hence, what oftentimes starts as a lark continues to become a spark.

People who know my ministry remember that just "as a lark" I was joking about putting glass elevators in our church steeple. That was not taken seriously by anyone at first, but out of it emerged the concept of the Tower of Hope which stands today with an elevator and offices. Once "as a lark" the thought was jokingly suggested that we make the entire church out of glass. And out of that "lark" emerged the "spark" that turned into the Crystal Cathedral. It is important that we come up with creative solutions to what appear to be unsolvable situations.

So let's play the possibility thinking game and apply it to the problem of wiping out the federal debt. We shall offer ten possibilities that can contribute to paying off the debt. You will probably come up with ten better ideas, but let these suggestions stimulate you to believe that *paying off the debt is possible*. At least the possibility will emerge as potentially viable enough so that the goal should be taken seriously. In view of the immense far-reaching value that could be secured by achieving a debt-free status, the burden would fall upon the scoffer to come up with a better idea. If we play this game, by the time we finish these possibilities, the real issue will not be if it is possible but why we should not take it seriously and exercise leadership to go for it.

Possibility One: Eliminate Government Waste

As Americans dedicated to paying off the national debt, let's first tackle it at the most critical area, the area of government waste. It is a highly documented fact that each year the government wastes billions of dollars, which contributes to growing deficits and larger and larger debts. Therefore, the first possibility we propose to pay off our national debt is cutting back government waste.

Some people will immediately reply, "The government

has been wasting money for centuries, ever since George Washington threw a silver dollar across the Potomac. You'll never get government to quit wasting money. You'll always have waste in the government; there is nothing you can do about it!"

Stop right there! That is a negative attitude! That type of thinking defeats you before you even get out of the starting gate. Remember, change starts with your attitude. Simply because it has been difficult to stop wasteful government spending in the past does not mean it cannot be done now. It is not a hopeless situation until we become hopeless people.

In 1981 President Reagan called on J. Peter Grace, chairman of W. R. Grace Company, to lead the Private Sector Survey on Cost Control, a commission that studied detailed ways in which the government could save money now being wasted. Peter Grace is chief executive officer of one of the top corporations in the world and has a reputation for guarding against waste in business operations.

One hundred sixty-one top executives staffed thirty-six major task forces at a cost of $75 million and produced 2,478 cost-cutting and revenue-enhancing recommendations that would save the government $424.4 billion in the first three years and $1.9 trillion per year by the year 2000. These findings were set out in a twenty-one-thousand-page report supported by 1.5 million pages of documentation, showing waste, inefficiencies, and mismanagement in the giant bureaucracy of our government. The entire cost of the project was paid by the private sector through donations of time and money. There was no cost to the government.

No human being knows more about waste in the American government than J. Peter Grace. After hearing that we were planning to write *The Power of Being Debt Free,* Grace agreed to meet with us. We sat in a wonderful little restaurant in Newport Beach, California, where he listened intently as we shared with him our concern over the debt we are incurring for our children and our dream of a debt-free America.

He wholeheartedly supported our goal and pointed out that rampant waste in government is a major problem that needs to be resolved immediately. Grace explained that the major aim of the president's Private Sector Survey on Cost Control was to force the government to run our nation as efficiently as American private enterprise would run its own businesses. "If America can do this," he said, "we will drastically reduce the deficit and debt."

Grace showed us the tremendous value of saving just one dollar right now. "Let's say I argue with a congressman about one dollar, but he won't take it out of the budget. I will ask him, 'Where will you get that dollar?' He would say, 'I'll borrow it.' What's the interest? Eleven percent. If that dollar stays in the budget the next year, he has to borrow last year's interest and this year's interest, as well as the original two dollars—one dollar for each year. The compounding calculation is that one wasteful dollar left in the budget today will amount to a cumulative seventy-one dollars in the national debt by the year 2000. Seventy-one dollars! Therefore, $100 billion in reduced government spending in the first year will equal a cumulative $4.1 trillion savings in the national debt by the year 2000, only fifteen years away."

Grace continued, "We found $424.4 billion in waste and inefficiencies that could be saved over the next three years. That's about $140 billion a year. Multiply that by seventy-one dollars and you've got $10 trillion! That's what we're talking about. If Congress will get with it and stop spouting off about things it knows are not true, then we'll save $10 trillion for ourselves and our grandchildren.

"There are 535 people in Congress, and I have said that two-thirds of them are clowns. The reason I say that is because they are clowning around with a terrible problem that faces not only us but our children and grandchildren who are going to have to pick up the tab for this terrible spending over the next fifty years. We're spending 25 percent more than we take in. Our $1.5 trillion debt is going up $175 billion a year. Our computer programs showed that the annual deficit in the year 2000 will be $1.966 trillion. Call it $2 trillion. The interest on the debt will be $1.5 trillion per year. We're passing that on. It means our freedoms will be gone. Instead of improving the quality of life in this country and making our nation stronger, we will be trapped into a terrible financial problem."

According to Grace, the government not only wastes $140 billion a year, but it also lacks critical information to collect the money owed to it.

"The government is owed $850 billion," he said to us, "but that money has never been aged. The government doesn't know whether it is due, overdue, or when it is due at all. Eight hundred and fifty billion dollars is three times the total taxes owed by all the taxpayers in America for three years! In addition to not knowing when the debt is owed, our government's computers are so obsolete that they are not interfaced with one another nor can they furnish the information needed. At least 50 percent of everything that one needs to run the government is not available to those who are making the decisions!" (Most of the government's computers are more than seven years old and cannot be serviced by the computer industry because of their age.)

The commission found that more than six thousand dead persons were still receiving checks regularly from the government. "Between the years 1980 and 1982," Grace said, "there was $14.6 billion paid out in false payments by the Social Security Administration, including payments to dead people. The families who received some of this $14.6 billion apparently forgot that the people had died!"

Fraud is another major problem in government, especially in the area of social programs. "There's at least $20 billion a year in fraud," said Grace. "When we worked with the Office of Management and Budget we asked, 'How many social programs are there?' They said, 'About 120 to 130.' But we found a book in Washington called, *Fat City: How to Get Yours.* We came back to the office and said, 'Look at this book! There are more social programs than 120 or 130.' We later found out that there are 963 different social programs, and you can get in 17 of them at the same time if you try hard enough.

"There are all kinds of fraud. The General Accounting Office just said it had discovered more than $1 billion in food stamp fraud. We don't need 963 social programs. We only need 10 or 20. There's a lot of fraud all through the government, and a lot of people in the bureaucracy are making their way in life by doling out money in both state and federal governments with the federal government picking up the tab."

Poor people are not getting the money that is allocated to them, according to Grace. His commission found that only thirty cents of each dollar allocated to help the poor actually reaches them. The rest is lost or used in the administration of the programs. "Where did the money go?" Grace asked. "It's siphoned off to the bureaucracy. The needy people don't need that kind of help!"

In his book *Burning Money* Grace tells of another case of fraud that the commission uncovered:

There was a contractor for the National Institute of Education who managed to do quite well at taxpayer expense. How? Let us count the ways: First, he held onto $71,000 he was supposed to pay to people attending a conference; then, he neglected to return another $25,000 in unused cash advances. Next, he used an undetermined amount of Institute money to support his other businesses. Afterward, he loaned over $100,000 of government money to friends and associates. Next, he overstated salaries by $23,000. Finally, this sterling citizen accepted, without comment, overpayments of $20,000 resulting from the Institute's inept accounting procedures.[1]

Inefficiency and poor management have led to some amusing but true stories reported in the media concerning the government's expenditure of our tax dollars. Mr. Grace asked us if we had heard the one about the $436 hammer which was identical to a $7 hammer in a local hardware store. In the same book, he gives the Defense Department's explanation.[2] Added to the basic $7 cost of the hammer was:

- $41 to pay general overhead costs for the engineering involved in mapping out the hammer problem. This included twelve minutes in secretarial time preparing the hammer purchase order, twenty-six minutes of management time spent on the hammer purchase, and two hours and thirty-six minutes the engineers spent on determining the hammer's specifications.
- $93 for the eighteen minutes it took for "mechanical subassembly" of the hammer, four hours for engineers to map out the hammer assembly process, ninety minutes spent by managers overseeing the hammer manufacturing process, sixty minutes for a project engineer to ensure the hammer was properly assembled, fifty-four minutes spent by quality-control engineers examining the hammer to ensure it did not have any defects, and seven hours and forty-eight minutes devoted to other support activities involved in assembling the hammer.
- $102 spent toward "manufacturing overhead."
- $37 for the sixty minutes the "spares repair department" spent gearing up for either repairing or finding parts should the hammer ever break.

- $2 for "material handling overhead," representing the payroll costs for the people to wrap the hammer and sent it out.
- $1 for wrapping paper and box.

This brought the subtotal of costs for the hammer to $283. This figure was increased by $90, representing the defense contractor's general administrative costs, and another $56 was added for a finder's fee for locating the specific hammer that fit the Navy's needs. Another $7 was added as the "capital cost of money" for the hammer purchase.

A Navy spokesman explained that large defense contractors are permitted to charge off general costs against all contracted items, and that in the case of relatively inexpensive items, these costs may appear disproportionately large. We have to agree; $436 for a $7 hammer does appear to be a "disproportionately large" price to pay.

Along with the $436 hammer, the military also paid $511 for a 60¢ light bulb and $100 for an aircraft simulator part that actually cost only 5¢ at a hardware store. For the simulator, that's a 200,000 percent markup!

But military officials are not the only generous people in the government or the only ones who lack control over their department. Inefficiency seems to be a trademark of the United States government.

The Veterans Administration's hospital construction staff of eight hundred employees is matched in the private sector with a work force of only fifty people. Bureaucracy in the VA causes a project to take seven years to complete compared to the private sector's two years. And it will cost four times as much.

Subsidized mortgage loans made by the government in 1982 often went to people who didn't need help to buy their homes. Most who received help had incomes of $20,000 to $40,000 a year, and 53 percent were affluent families with several earning over $50,000 a year.

Some of these items may seem trivial, but they are indicative of a philosophy that leads to overspending by billions of dollars year in and year out.

Civil service and military personnel are also getting their share of government dollars through excessively generous pension plans. According to Grace in a letter to the president, the civil service and military retirement systems provide three to six times, respectively, the benefits of the best pension plans in the private sector. The government's employees also retire at an earlier age with the added luxury of having their pension funds indexed for inflation, something that is virtually unheard of in the business world. Is it any wonder that most government employees speak disparagingly of the findings of the Grace Commission?

Representatives and senators also enjoy the benefits of government service. According to the National Taxpayers Union, thirty-six members of Congress could receive more than $1 million each from federal pension benefits during their lifetime if they leave office after their current terms expire. Members of Congress who elect to participate in the retirement system contribute 8 percent of their salary and become eligible for benefits after five years of service. According to the taxpayer group, the federal plan far exceeds the benefits of the typical private company.

Another added plus for the elected elite is that they are allowed to eat in one of the posh restaurants found at NASA, the Department of Labor, the State Department, the Pentagon, and other agencies. A lunch that usually costs $10.00 at a Washington restaurant will cost only $3.50 or $4.00 in one of these government-subsidized restaurants. In 1981, these restaurants cost $2.9 million to operate, but they brought in only $500,000. The subsidy per meal was $12.00, compared to 50¢ per meal paid out to food stamp recipients.

In cash management, budgeting improvement, and accounting measures the government could save more than $30 billion in three years. Examples of improvements that could be made are in the areas of revamping the government's system of "first in, first out" payment of bills. When the government receives a bill, it pays immediately, although the bill may not be due for six to eight months in the future. By using electronic fund transfers instead of direct mail in paying bills and in sending salary checks to government employees, the government could save hundreds of millions of dollars over the next three years. The Postal Service, for instance, issues 22.4 million checks annually through the Treasury Department at a cost of $1.01 per check. Commercial banks would provide the same service for 10¢ per check. If taxes collected from import duties and from the alcohol and tobacco industries were paid electronically instead of by mail, hundreds of millions of dollars could be saved.

If the government would manage by the following principles, it could save $30 billion in the next three years:

- pay bills when they are due and not earlier unless there is sufficient beneficial reason to do so;
- immediately deposit checks received;
- keep as little money as possible in accounts that do not earn interest and as much as possible in interest-bearing accounts.

The list of inefficiencies, waste, and mismanagement in government seems endless. In almost every kind of agency, some waste seems to be apparent.

In the Department of Labor there is virtually no control over long-distance telephone usage. One regional office did restrict long distance use and was able to save $1 million per year, but other offices have not followed suit. In the private sector, one telephone for every employee is considered to be an unusually high telephone-to-employee ratio. But in the Department of Labor the ratio is nine to seven, more telephones than employees. And 90 percent of those are more expensive multiline phones, whereas 30 percent or less is usually considered adequate in private industry.

If you were to write a letter to the director of the Health and Human Services Department, your letter would be physically handled by fifty-five to sixty people. More than forty-five days would pass before you would receive an answer. Compare this to an average of five days if you wrote a major corporation in the private sector.

If you want to patent or trademark something, your letter will be one of twenty thousand arriving daily at the United States Office of Patents and Trademarks. Your letter will be filed by hand before taking its place in a backlog of applications that are now two years behind in being acted upon.

The government as a whole should be entitled to major corporate discounts for travel because its work force is larger than any private corporation in America. However, more than $2.4 billion, or 50 percent of the government's travel allowance, was used to pay for travel tickets at full-fare rates. If all arrangements could be made through centralized or regional agencies which made an all-out effort to secure low-cost air fares, the government could save $984 million in three years.

Many public power utilities throughout America receive subsidies from the government so that recipients are charged less than one-half what those persons receiving power from privately run public utility plants are charged. Those who pick up the difference are taxpayers in other states.

The maintenance and construction of dams and waterways for commercial traffic cost $850 million in 1981. Only $24 million was collected from those who used the waterways. The rest was paid by public tax dollars.

The stories of government waste can go on and on. There can be little doubt that government waste, mismanagement, and inefficiency greatly contribute to our rising national debt.

According to the Grace Commission, one-third of all taxes are consumed by waste and inefficiency in the federal government. Another one-third of all taxes escapes collection as the underground economy grows in direct proportion to tax increases. This places additional pressure on law-abiding taxpayers. With two-thirds of income taxes wasted or not collected, 100 percent of what is collected is absorbed *by interest on the federal debt* and by federal government contributions to transfer payments. All individual income tax revenues are gone before one nickel is spent on services that taxpayers expect from their government.

Unless something is done to stop government waste, the Grace Commission projects that the national debt will reach $13 trillion by the year 2000 and the annual deficits will approach $2 trillion. Those figures are astronomical! You ask, "What can possibly be done?" There are many answers.

At present, less than 25 percent of the 2,478 cost-cutting, revenue-enhancing savings recommendations of the Grace Commission have been implemented. If the remaining 75 percent are swiftly put into action, the debt will be dramatically reduced. Data Resources, Incorporated, probably the most reputable economics and computer data forecasting firm in the United States, projects that the federal debt, with the Grace Commission recommendations implemented, will equal $2.5 trillion by the year 2000 instead of $13 trillion. That is a savings to the taxpayers of $10.5 trillion!

There are many areas where relief in government spending is already being felt. The National Taxpayers Union lobby in Washington has saved the taxpayers millions of dollars by being a diligent watchdog restraining Congress's spending sprees. The federal government has set up a toll-free hotline for anyone who sees blatant misuse and waste of tax dollars and wishes to report it. This system has already saved $20 million in its first few years of operation. Do you have a complaint against waste? Report it today at (800) 424-5454 for those outside the Washington, D.C., area or at (202) 633-6987 for those in the Washington vicinity. If you call after hours, a recorder will take your message and someone will get back to you.

In the Defense Department, Inspector-General Joseph H. Sherick is overseeing a three-year drive against waste, fraud, and abuse. Already his investigation has uncovered $6.3 billion in waste and fraud. Most results from defective material or parts sold to the department at outrageous prices. So far his work has retrieved $2.9 billion, and more money is expected to be saved in the future.

Although groups and task forces are beginning to combat government waste, there is still no sutstitute in our electoral system for direct pressure on the House and Senate to be accountable to a concerned and aware public. You can write your elected officials. Share this book with ten people and have them get involved by writing their representative and senators. Let it be known to these elected officials that you will vote for the ones who do the most to secure our economic future.

Eliminating government waste is just one of the positive possibilities for paying off the federal debt, but it is the first step we must take to meet this challenge. It is also the most important step because it will have the greatest impact on the debt and will not cost taxpayers anything.

Our government can learn a lot from the old Far Eastern parable.

A wife came to her husband and said, "I would like to buy a new bed cover."

The husband answered, "What will you do with the old bed cover?"

The wife replied, "I will cut it up and make new pillow covers."

"What will you do with the old pillow covers?" he asked.

"I will use them for dust cloths," the wife answered.

"What will you do with the old dust cloths?" he questioned.

She answered, "I will tie them together and make a new mop."

He asked again, "What will you do with the old mop?"

"Oh," she said, "I will chop it up, mix it with ashes, and use it to stuff the holes in the outside of the house."

The husband was silent. Finally he spoke. "All right. You can buy a new bed cover."

7

Ten Ways to Accomplish the Impossible—Part Two

After speaking with Peter Grace and studying his commission's recommendations, we were encouraged by the tremendous amount of money that could be saved by taking steps to eliminate government waste, inefficiencies, and mismanagement. But you might ask, "Where is the guarantee that Congress and the federal government will not fall back into wasteful spending sprees and mismanagement of taxpayers' money?"

Currently the way Congress is set up resembles a situation in which 535 people have joint access to a major credit card—all with the same account number. Everyone can spend as much as he or she wants, but when the bill is tallied, each person will owe exactly 1/535 of the bill, regardless of how much he or she personally spent.

It is not hard to imagine what happens. Everyone tries to get more at everyone else's expense. That is exactly what is happening in our government today.

We need to set limits on how much we can spend. Almost every business has some limitations on the amount of money it can spend. We propose a legal limit to federal spending.

Possibility Two: Set Up a Legal Spending Limitation

A constitutional amendment requiring the federal government to balance the budget on a yearly basis would impose limits on the amount of money Congress could spend. Congress would not be allowed to raise the debt ceiling and borrow money to fund pet projects and please special interest groups. However, a balanced budged amendment could have a provision for it to be waived in times of national emergencies, such as war or natural disaster.

The Constitution provides the following procedures for adding an amendment: "The Congress, whenever two-thirds of both Houses shall deem it necessary, shall propose Amendments to this Constitution, or, on the Application of the Legislatures of two-thirds of the several States, shall call a Convention for proposing Amendments, which, in either Case, shall be valid . . . when ratified by the Legislatures of three-fourths of the several States."

In other words, there are two ways to amend the Constitution. First, Congress may propose amendments. This is how all twenty-six existing amendments to the Constitution have started. The second way is for the states to call for a constitutional convention to propose and discuss amendments. When two-thirds of the states request a convention, it must be held. Once proposed—either by Congress or by a constitutional convention—an amendment must be ratified by three-fourths of the states to become a part of the Constitution.

In 1981 a constitutional amendment to balance the budget and limit federal taxes was drafted. While it was approved in the United States Senate by a wide margin, it received less than the two-thirds majority vote required for passage in the House of Representatives. A new amendment called the Balanced Budget Tax Limitation Amendment has been introduced in the 98th Congress and is still pending.

In the meantime, a movement to call for a constitutional convention is growing in strength. Thirty-two states have already voted to call for such a convention in order to produce a constitutional amendment requiring a balanced budget. Since a two-thirds majority of the states is required, only two more states need to vote in favor of this initiative in order for there to be a convention.

A major criticism of a constitutional convention, however, is that while it might be called to discuss a balanced budget amendment, it would open the door to a discussion of any amendment. Extremists, for instance, might want to question the Bill of Rights or make other proposals that would severely limit our freedoms or change the character of the Constitution as we know it today. To help ease the fear of a runaway constitutional convention open to any subject, a limit of one issue—the balanced budget amendment—should be imposed on the convention. A specific time frame, such as 120 days, could also be appointed for deliberation on this issue.[1]

The Nobel-Prize-winning economist Milton Friedman is the champion and chief advocate of such a constitutional amendment. He discussed his feelings concerning this proposal with us.

"If you had asked me ten years ago what I thought our chances were of passing a constitutional amendment, I would have replied maybe one in ten. But now with only two more states required for the two-thirds majority, I think we have a better than even chance that such a constitutional convention could take place in the next two years," he said.

We need some kind of legal insurance to limit government spending permanently. While the details of such a permanent limitation are being worked out, we must take steps to limit spending immediately.

Possibility Three: Impose an Across-the-Board Spending Freeze

Strong support is growing in Congress for a proposal to freeze government spending for the next three years. A spending freeze would limit any *increase* in funds to existing programs for the next three years. Their funding would not be cut back; it simply would not be increased.

Supporters of such a freeze say that if spending is held at current levels as the economy continues to grow, revenues will increase and deficits will therefore decline. When revenues catch up with the existing spending level, we will have a balanced budget. Over the past fifteen years, revenues and spending have both increased almost every year. It is estimated that if spending is held in check, it will take about three years for the rise in revenues to eliminate the yearly deficit and balance the budget.

An across-the-board spending freeze would be an effective way of eliminating the deficit now without much hardship, rather than paying for the cumulative deficits later at a greater cost. A balanced budget would be achieved without cuts in current services and without increases in taxes.

As inflation has slowed, the costs of goods and services have stabilized and, in some cases, have declined. Oil prices have dropped from $34 to $26.50 a barrel. Steel, lumber, and other building materials were less expensive at the end of 1984 than they were at the end of 1983. Since the government can complete many projects at lower interest rates with cheaper-priced materials, increases to various programs only encourage waste.

Politicians struggled to communicate the effectiveness of an across-the-board spending freeze in the presidential election. The *Washington Post* reported that Senator Ernest F. Hollings of South Carolina was making all the obligatory

Federal Spending Freeze

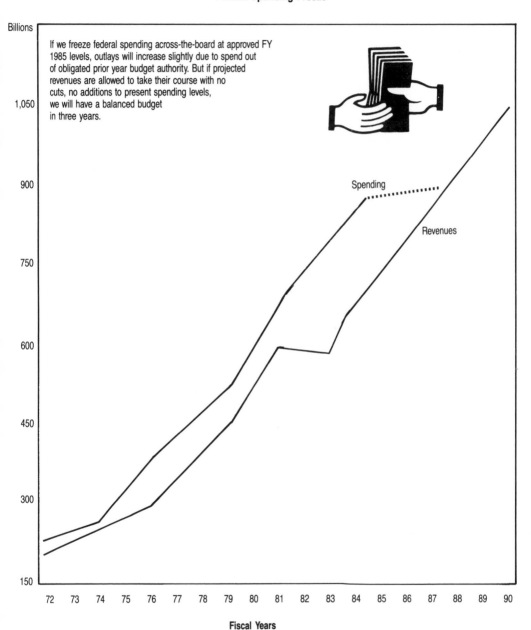

Billions

If we freeze federal spending across-the-board at approved FY 1985 levels, outlays will increase slightly due to spend out of obligated prior year budget authority. But if projected revenues are allowed to take their course with no cuts, no additions to present spending levels, we will have a balanced budget in three years.

1,050

900

Spending

Revenues

750

600

450

300

150

72 73 74 75 76 77 78 79 80 81 82 83 84 85 86 87 88 89 90

Fiscal Years

stops on the 1984 Democratic presidential circuit, wooing blacks, the aged, the poor, and the struggling middle class with the unconventional promise that he would do nothing for their cherished social programs. In other words, he promised a total freeze on all spending. Right across the board.

People across America are putting their support behind this proposal. The *Wall Street Journal* disclosed the popular reaction to this possibility.

> There is a considerable momentum building for a freeze in Congress. . . . A spending freeze is fair. It simply holds the line while allowing re-allocation as necessary within the total. . . . A spending freeze would be exactly the sort of bold stroke for which people are yearning. The signal that a spending freeze would send to both Main Street and Wall Street would be incomparable. The specter of extraordinary deficits, which the pundits seem to agree is the only barrier to a steady, even robust economic recovery, would evaporate under a spending freeze.[2]

Recently the Senate Budget Committee came within two votes of passing a spending freeze proposal. If Americans can unite to accept this small sacrifice today, we can prevent a major catastrophe from happening in the future.

Possibility Four: Permit a Line-Item Veto

Currently, the president has the option of allowing an entire bill passed by both houses of Congress to become law or of vetoing the entire bill. It's all or nothing. A line-item veto would give the president the power to veto or negate any portion of a bill while approving the balance of it. This would give the president greater ability to eliminate government spending that is wasteful or favors special interest groups.

Popular bills that are sure to be passed and approved

by the president frequently contain many amendments un-related to the main bill which ordinarily would not pass on their own if presented as independent bills. Representatives and senators have found this to be an attractive way to please special interest groups, and so it has become a much-abused practice that leads to government waste. The president and members of Congress alike, although they recognize the abuse and waste of these special attachments to major bills, are forced to approve them in order to pass the major bill itself.

For example, suppose the president supports a major bill calling for an increase in Medicare and social security payments to the elderly. But attached to the bill are twenty unrelated items calling for a variety of government subsidies such as low-interest loans to a major building contractor in one state or a subsidy of power for another state. While the president recognizes that the majority of Americans will not benefit from subsidized power in one state, or low-interest loans in another state, he is powerless to do anything about it if he wants to pass the primary bill.

A line-item veto would give the president the power to delete from the bill those lines that are unfair to the majority of Americans. The president is the only elected official who is voted into office by all Americans. Therefore he is not as susceptible to the pressure of powerful lobbies in individual states as senators and representatives are. Rather, he is responsible to the majority of the people.

Congress would, of course, be able to override a line-item veto with a two-thirds majority vote just as it can now override the veto of an entire bill.

A line-item veto would give the president the power to veto anything that he felt was wasteful government spending, and thereby help save each dollar to be put into effective use. With a line-item veto we will start to see results immediately!

Possibility Five: Establish a Federal Debt Reduction Bank

We propose that the Congress of the United States establish and charter a Federal Debt Reduction Bank that has as its one objective to be the guardian of the finanical future of unborn American citizens. How irresponsible would we be in our own personal debt expansion if we had no tough lending institution looking over our shoulders every time we wanted to borrow more money? If we could borrow money from a bank without the need to present a financial statement showing our assets, liabilities, and our ability to handle the financial obligations, is it not likely that we would quickly borrow money irresponsibly and recklessly?

Our government has operated without any fiscal restraint for more than two hundred years. The Federal Debt Reduction Bank of the United States would monitor funds, collect funds, make payments, and manage funds arising from all sources to pay off the debt. The monies received could not be used for anything else.

At present Congress and/or the president have the power to simply expand the federal debt without having a financial review of the government's ability to pay off the increased debt. Just as we have a Supreme Court to ultimately pass judgment on legal cases, does it not merit consideration to establish a Federal Debt Reduction Bank of the United States for the purpose of passing judgment on the government's ability to repay its indebtedness? The Federal Debt Reduction Bank would actually assume the liabilities of the government and be responsible for paying off the debt. In turn it would hold title to the physical assets of the government in the name of the people. The collateral in the bank could be government lands and properties.

The Federal Debt Reduction Bank of the United States would have the responsibility of making sure that elected officials did not become reckless and irresponsible in their approval of budgets. The bank, along with its board of directors consisting of nonelected persons, would ensure that politicians could not manipulate the budget to strengthen their chances of re-election at the expense of future generations.

Since the Federal Debt Reduction Bank would agree to take over the liability of the government's $1.8 trillion debt, the income potential of the country would have to be carefully studied. A repayment schedule, including interest and principal payments, would need to be approved by Congress. According to the Hudson Institute study, mentioned in chapter 2, the federal debt could be eliminated by as early as the year 2005 if this were done.

The Federal Debt Reduction Bank would assume liabilities of the government debt under the following provisions:

1. The Congress of the United States could not incur any new debt without the bank's approval.

2. In emergency situations Congress could discuss with the Federal Debt Reduction Bank temporary loans with predetermined obligations to repay the principal over an agreed-upon period of time, not to exceed our own generation.

The Federal Debt Reduction Bank could be the managing force to channel the funds that come from a multitude of sources. This would assure us that specific funds allocated for the repayment of the debt would not be siphoned off to meet the needs of other programs but would be used solely to help reduce our $1.836 trillion debt obligation.

What would this do to the morale of our country if we knew we were on a program that would gradually, dollar by dollar, reduce our federal debt and at the same time promise a bright and prosperous future for our children and grand-children?

Challenged to seek further solutions to repay the national debt, we sought the advice of the renowned economist, Milton Friedman. From our discussion with him came another positive possibility.

Possibility Six: Increase Revenues through Change in the Tax System

"When your outgo exceeds your income," John Joseph's father told him, "it's the upstart of your downfall." If we are to pay off the national debt, we must decrease outgo, increase income, or both. Therefore, possibility number six is that we should increase revenues so that the government has more money coming in.

It would seem as if the most obvious way to increase revenues is to increase taxes. Yet Milton Friedman and others say that the best way to increase revenues is to eliminate the entire existing federal income tax structure and impose a true flat tax. While the current tax structure has sixteen tax brackets graduated from 11 to 50 percent according to one's income, a flat tax would designate an equal percentage rate that every citizen would pay in taxes. Dr. Friedman recommends a rate between 17 and 20 percent, while other proponents recommend rates as high as 30 percent.

With a flat tax, the people making $10,000 a year would pay the same percentage of their incomes as people making $100,000 a year. In addition to the equal percentage rate, various deductions that are currently available would be eliminated. The amount of money one could earn before paying any tax at all would be raised from the current level of $3,400 to almost $10,000 in some proposals.

Opponents of the flat tax claim that the tax burden would shift to the poor. But according to Friedman, every class of society would benefit. The poor and middle classes would pay less taxes due to higher personal exemptions and lower rates, while the rich would pay more tax but actually be better off because money they spend now for non-productive tax shelters could be freed up to use in more productive areas.

But how would a flat tax actually yield as much or more revenue as the present system?

In *Tyranny of the Status Quo,* which he wrote with his wife, Rose, Friedman explains the process.

> The reason is that although the tax rates are steeply graduated on paper, the law is riddled with loopholes and special provisions, so that the high rates become window dressing. The income tax does indeed "soak the rich," but that soaking does not yield much revenue to the government. It rather takes the form of inducing the rich to acquire costly tax shelters and rearrange their affairs in other ways that will minimize actual tax payments. There is a very large wedge between the cost to the taxpayer and the revenue to the government. The magnitude of that wedge was illustrated by the reduction in 1981 of the top rate on so-called unearned income from 70 to 50 percent. Despite an ensuing recession, the taxes actually paid at rates of 50 percent and above went up, not down as a result.[3]

In late November 1984, the Treasury Department proposed that President Reagan consider a modified flat tax that would eliminate many deductions and consolidate the existing sixteen tax brackets into three: 15 percent, 25 percent, and 35 percent. If passed, this modified flat tax would represent the most significant overhaul of the system since the income tax was first instituted more than seventy years ago.

Raising revenue by changing the tax structure to a flat tax is a viable option. But another possible way to increase revenue might be to actually lower taxes altogether. "Taxes are always a negative incentive," economist Arthur Laffer told us.

When the amount of taxes a person needs to pay is decreased, he will be encouraged to work harder and keep more. When taxes are lowered, people are motivated to earn as much as they possibly can. For instance, a person in the 40 percent tax bracket might have the opportunity to earn an additional $10,000 if he works longer hours or increases his sales. But after taxes, he keeps only $6,000. His motivation to earn that additional income is clearly less than it would be if he were to keep $8,000.

If we increase motivation to work by lowering taxes, our country will see an increase in productivity. This increase in productivity will provide a broader base from which the government can collect revenues. The result is, for instance, that the government is better off with 20 percent of $200,000 ($40,000) than with 30 percent of $100,000 ($30,000).

Arthur Laffer is a strong proponent of this concept. He explained to us more fully how motivation plays an important role in productivity and how taxes and government programs affect motivation.

"When it comes to taxes," he said, "you know exactly what people will try not to do. They will try not to report taxable income. But you won't know how they will avoid reporting that taxable income. They may use tax shelters. They may participate in the underground economy in which all work is done for cash and all goods are sold for cash so that the transaction cannot be recorded. But you know they will try to avoid reporting their taxable income.

"However, if the government subsidizes a certain activity, you know exactly what people will do. They will try to do whatever gives them the subsidy. When you tax something, you get less of it. When you subsidize something, you get more of it."

Dr. Laffer went on to explain that the federal government is basically "taxing work output and employment and subsidizing nonwork, leisure, and unemployment. It should come as no shock to anyone why we are getting so little work out of those who are employed and such nonwork and leisure from those who are not employed.

"If you want people to be fully and productively employed and wealthy, you should provide them the incentives to do so. It just doesn't make sense to say, 'Raising taxes on workers and producers is going to give us more workers and producers.'"

According to Laffer, if people can gain more from being unemployed and staying on government programs or from not reporting income, then they naturally will do so. This, in turn, raises deficits through the subsidy of more social programs. In Laffer's opinion, the deficits exist largely because the tax system stifles incentives for people to work and pay fair and reasonable taxes.

"Let me give one example which illustrates this point," Laffer said. "The maximum legal social welfare benefits a family of four living in Los Angeles today can receive is $1,147 per month. This assumes no one in the family is working and includes food stamps, medical benefits, and other programs. Then let's assume that one adult who can work decides to do so and earns $1,300 a month, from which is deducted employee payroll tax, federal income tax, social security, and state income tax. After taxes, this family is actually earning less than if it had stayed on welfare. The total spending power of the family of four actually declines. How much would you work if you knew you could earn more money by simply staying home? How much would you work if every time you went into the office, instead of getting a check you got a bill?"

"I dream of a debt-free society," concluded Dr. Laffer. "And the only way we can get there is through growth and prosperity."

The point is that in order to pay off the debt, the government should increase revenue. It would be presumptuous of us to recommend how to do it—raise income taxes, lower income taxes, or scrap the existing system and institute a flat tax. We'll leave that to the economists and politicians. But we do need to increase government revenue.

It is also important to simplify the tax system. Our current system is so complex that our best thinkers spend their time on developing ways to reduce their own and their corporations' taxes. In the process they are not productive; they are not creating new inventions and ideas for the twenty-first century. They are distracted by nonproductive work—tax reduction—from creative, productive, positive contributions to society.

In addition to increasing revenue through changing the income tax structure, perhaps special taxes could be levied on industries that cost our nation money in various ways.

The surgeon general, C. Everett Koop, has pointed out that billions of dollars are spent on health care every year. Dr. Jonathan Fielding, president of United States Corporate Health, says that Americans spend the equivalent of 11 percent of the nation's gross national product on health-related costs. More than a billion dollars a day is spent on hospital care in America.

How much of this enormous health care cost is directly related to problems caused by smoking and excessive drinking? It has been reported that each pack of cigarettes costs the American taxpayer three dollars in health care. What is the cost to America's productivity due to alcoholism? An increased tax on these industries' products should be considered. So far, however, powerful tobacco and liquor lobbyists in Washington have successfully avoided tax bills which would impose higher taxes on their products.

What other positive tax measures could we legislate in Congress? Perhaps we should institute a tax on luxury items such as they do in some European countries. Perhaps we should institute a specialized tax on those industries that harm or pollute the environment or add to the government's financial burden in some way. There are many specialized taxes that should be considered to reduce the federal deficit.

Possibility Seven: Lower Interest Rates

Economist Gary Shilling, co-author with Kiril Sokoloff of *Is Inflation Ending? Are You Ready?* (McGraw-Hill), told us that, historically, real interest rates have only been 2 to 3 percent higher than the rate of inflation. The real interest rate is the difference between what you earn on your money and what inflation eats away. For example, if you earn 15 percent on your money but inflation is at 12 percent, your real interest rate of return is 3 percent.

But, Dr. Shilling pointed out, currently the real interest rate is more than 9 percent. As of late 1984, the average yield on a thirty-year bond was nearly 14 percent, while inflation was at a mere 4 percent. The reason for this unusual spread, according to Shilling, is that the Federal Reserve Board and investors are afraid that inflation will come roaring back in the future. But many economists question if we will ever return to the days of hyperinflation such as in the 1970s.

Many of the elements contributing to such hyperinflation have drastically changed. An oil crisis, like that of 1974, is no longer the major threat it once was. Some oil analysts say the United States has a thirty-to-forty-year oil reserve which it can easily tap in the event of an oil embargo. OPEC nations produce oil at a cost of $2.10 to $2.60 a barrel. In early 1984 the price of oil fell from $36 to $26 a barrel. This exorbitant profit margin is a major contributor to worldwide inflation. As the price of oil declines, inflation will also decline. Our development of alternative energy sources and our conservation of energy have also weakened the price of oil and the impact it makes on inflation.

In the last few years we have seen the rise in prices of speculative investments such as gold, silver, and real estate, primarily bought by speculators and investors. Some wanted insurance against inflation. Others thought prices would continue to skyrocket. But we are beginning to see cracks in the markets for real estate, gold, silver, diamonds, and other speculative commodities. The price of a flawless diamond has fallen from $60,000 a carat to $12,000. Gold has dropped from $860 an ounce to the $300 range. Silver plummeted from $50 an ounce to $5. Other raw commodities, such as lumber, steel, copper, and aluminum, no longer include in their costs inflation hedges. The world is becoming more of a free market with low-cost imports flowing into the United States from Korea, Japan, Indonesia, and other countries.

With increased competition in the world markets, the prices of goods reflect more of the true cost of taking them out of the ground, making them into products, and shipping and delivering them. The price-conscious competitor is the one who gets the business.

As inflation slows, the Federal Reserve Board should remove the inflation hedge that is built into the high real interest rates. Dr. Shilling told us, "If we are right about a 3 percent inflation forecast, treasury bond yields could fall to 6 percent and treasury bills to even less."

What effect will lower interest rates have on the deficits and debt? With $1.836 trillion in interest-bearing federal debt outstanding, each 1 percent decline in interest rates would eventually reduce the amount paid in interest on the national debt by $1.8 billion. "From a peak of $120 billion in fiscal 1985, net interest cost would fall to about $50 billion by fiscal 1990," said Dr. Shilling. "Combining this reduction with no real growth in federal outlays, the deficit would all but disappear in fiscal 1988."

"Perhaps even more incredible," Shilling continued, "is the fact that if interest rates continued at those lower levels and other real outlays stayed flat in real terms beyond fiscal 1988, federal receipts would outrun outlays and meaningful and growing surpluses would result.''

According to Dr. Shilling, with lower interest rates our deficit would plunge from $200 billion to zero in only three years. After that time we would have a surplus that could be used to pay off the federal debt.

8

★

Ten Ways to Accomplish
the Impossible—Part Three

Our government and economic leaders can explore a myriad of traditional, mainstream problem-solving solutions to pay off the national debt. They include eliminating government waste, implementing a constitutional amendment to limit government spending, imposing an across-the-board spending freeze, using a line-item veto, establishing a Federal Debt Reduction Bank, increasing government revenues through a change in the tax system, and lowering interest rates. But our possibility thinking game can take us beyond these obvious answers to our nation's great financial predicament.

As we let our imagination run freely, what other creative problem-solving possibilities can we dream up?

Possibility Eight: Sell or Lease Government Assets

Many government-owned properties could be sold or leased to the private sector with the income going to the Federal Debt Reduction Bank. Obviously this sale or lease needs to be done in such a way as to avoid exploitation of the environment. Of course there is potential for abuse or problems. But this just underscores a fundamental principle of possibility thinking: there is something wrong with every good idea. Don't reject an idea just because it has a problem with it. Every positive idea needs to be analyzed and dissected. Separate the negative part of the idea, isolate it, and eliminate it. Then release the positive element of the idea for its fullest potential.

Many government assets could be sold to raise large sums of money. Consider federal buildings and the current value of these properties. Does it make sense for the government, a nonprofit institution, to hold title to office buildings? As pastor of a church, I can say it does not pay for a nonprofit organization to hold title to apartment buildings or office buildings that have to compete with those built and operated by for-profit corporations. The simple reason is that for-profit corporations can deduct the interest on the mortgages as an expense as well as depreciate the value of the properties, all of which translates into a stronger bottom line after taxes for the corporation. Perhaps it would make better sense for the government to sell its office buildings to profit-making corporations in the private sector and then lease them back.

In addition, the government could consider leasing equipment and property it owns to the private sector. For instance, the government could protect special parcels of land by leasing them rather than selling them.

Services could also be leased. For years we have tried to get the Marine Band to perform at one of our church services, but we have been told repeatedly that the band is not allowed to play at a sectarian church service unless the president or vice-president of the United States is in attendance. We would happily make a gift to the government if we could "rent" the band for certain religious functions.

There was a time when the state of California did not allow public school buildings to be rented for church purposes. That was until the state had an urgent need for cash. Today, public schools that used to stand empty on Sunday mornings are now rented to churches for their Sunday services. The citizens of the state benefit and the congregations benefit. It is a "win-win" situation.

Are there ships or other vessels that the government could charter to corporations and private groups for seminars at sea? Undoubtedly many unused government properties, equipment, and services could be leased or sold to the private sector and generate billions of dollars to help pay off the national debt.

In a recent discussion with former President Gerald Ford concerning the elimination of the national debt, we brought up the topic of charitable gifts. "Do you realize," I asked the former president, "that in 1983 the American people contributed $65 billion to charity? Why couldn't we solicit volunteer gifts to help pay off the federal debt?"

"Well," he said, "that is a new approach. Maybe we could offer a tax deduction to people who make gifts to reduce the debt."

We were shocked. We assumed that any gifts to the federal government were currently deductible from income taxes. The fact is that they are not. In addition, we were not sure how much cash was available in the hands of Americans to give charitably to the government. To find out, we asked financial expert John Templeton.

Again we were in for a shock as Templeton nonchalantly told us the amount of liquid cash available. "Not counting real estate, stocks, or long-term bonds, there is $2.3 trillion in cash or financial instruments in the hands of the American people. This is more money than the entire available supply of stocks and warrants on the New York and American stock exchanges and the NASDAQ [National Association of Securities Dealers Automated Quotation] over-the-counter securities system."

Encouraged by this report, we came up with our next solution.

Possibility Nine: Provide Tax Incentives and Solicit Voluntary Contributions

Where did $65 billion in contributions to charity come from last year? How was it raised? It was contributed by people who were motivated to give money to a project or organization they believed in. If $65 billion was raised for charity last year, how much more could be raised by the people of this country if they knew that their gifts would help make America financially stable? Are we so jaded, so cynical that we do not believe that our fellow citizens would not share the same sense of sacrifice and devotion as our founding fathers who pledged their lives, fortunes, and honor for their freedom?

We feel confident that this may be one of the best solutions that we have yet presented, for we believe that the American people are generous and grateful for the terrific opportunities they have inherited by being citizens of the United States. We propose that $20 billion a year could be raised from caring and concerned individuals. Billions of dollars in benefits through Medicare, social security, and aid to the homeless and underprivileged were distributed in 1984. Why can't we contribute voluntarily, not just by heavy taxation, to help pay for these important programs?

What price can we put on our freedom? How much would each one of us be willing to give if we knew it would secure that same freedom for our children and grandchildren? We believe that many people would be willing to give money if they knew it was specifically earmarked for a fund that would help pay off the federal debt. The Federal Debt Reduction Bank could receive all monies in a special account that would let everyone know that their gifts were not being wasted by excessive government spending.

I have raised millions of dollars in cash gifts. People love to contribute large amounts of money to great causes.

In the building of the Crystal Cathedral, we received seven gifts of over $1 million. I am convinced that there are hundreds, perhaps thousands, of persons in America who would be willing to make gifts of more than $1 million if they knew their money would be secured in a bank that guaranteed the management of our country's indebtedness.

Is it unrealistic to think that there are potential gifts to the federal government in the billion-dollar bracket? And what about the millions of small gifts that could be raised? We believe this idea has countless possibilities. For a start, here are a few.

A Supertelethon

Imagine a live television program from Washington, D.C., hosted by our country's most respected politicians, the president, and famous entertainers that had as its sole objective to raise a certain amount of dollars to help repay the federal debt.

In 1984, Jerry Lewis raised $32 million in only twenty-four hours during a telethon for the Muscular Dystrophy Association. What a fantastic possibility a supertelethon would be to help pay off the national debt! It could last for a week, and private corporations could sponsor it to help pay for the air time, advertising, and production costs. All fifty states would have a role to play in raising funds. The personal involvement of hundreds of thousands of Americans would stimulate incredible momentum. It would help bring the country together to achieve a common goal. A financial upswing of confidence would also stimulate creativity and productivity to expand our national net worth to a degree that is unimaginable.

Even with possible large gifts, in the million- and billion-dollar range, we know that most organizations continue to be supported by the millions of people who give smaller donations. The same is true with our federal government today. It is not the rich people who support our nation with taxes but the average person who gives his or her share. We know that millions of people would want to give their smaller gifts to the government to help repay the federal debt, and the results would be overwhelming.

The Walk of Freedom

More than ten thousand people proudly donated five hundred dollars each to have a window in the Crystal Cathedral dedicated to them or the person of their choice. Today, we are in the process of raising an endowment fund for the cathedral that will be used to maintain the beauty of the gardens and grounds for generations to come. We are raising the money through what we call the "Walk of Faith." These are steppingstones around the property that have inscribed on them the name and favorite Bible verse of the donor who gave two thousand dollars toward this fund. These stones form a lovely mile-long walk throughout the twenty-acre campus of the cathedral. The Walk of Faith not only serves as a successful fund-raising campaign, but it also becomes a spiritual treat for everyone who visits the cathedral.

Perhaps the government could establish a "Walk of Freedom" to raise funds to help pay off the debt. For a two-thousand- or five-hundred-dollar gift individuals would have their names, or the names of their loved one, inscribed on a plaque or a steppingstone that would be placed somewhere in Washington, D.C. These could adorn the Capitol gardens or the grounds around the monuments or other important sites in the city, and the millions of visitors in years to come would be inspired by them.

Incentives to give are very important in any fund-raising campaign. The incentives the government could offer are endless.

Recognition on Currency and Stamps

With all due respect to George Washington, Abraham Lincoln, and some of our country's other great leaders, no law states that only their faces may appear on America's currency or that pictures on currency can't change from time to time. In consideration of major contributions of several million dollars, donors could be recognized and thanked by their fellow citizens through an act of Congress so that the donor's face would appear on a determined number of one-dollar bills, five-dollar bills, ten-dollar bills, even one-hundred-dollar bills. The largest bill in circulation today is a one-hundred-dollar bill. Wouldn't it be possible to print two-hundred-dollar, five-hundred-dollar, one-thousand-dollar, and ten-thousand-dollar bills in honor of those Americans who led us out of our national debt crisis?

Postage stamps could also be printed with the names and faces of donors who greatly contributed to our financial freedom. Private and public corporations and institutions could also be honored for their fund-raising efforts.

Highways and Parks

What federal highways and parks remain unnamed? Thousands of highways that crisscross America's countryside are designated only by a number or letter. Why couldn't they bear the names of persons or institutions who made efforts to reduce the debt? Beautiful countryside parks could be named after the people who campaigned together to secure our nation's financial freedom.

Today, between the Capitol Building and the Washington Monument spreads the magnificent Washington Mall. An inspiring Gallery of National Heroes could line the marvelous plaza, bearing in granite the slogans that are the foundation of our country along with the names of the people who made major gifts to win an all-out war against the nation's greatest enemy, the federal debt. Let us give living Americans in the twentieth century the opportunity to make a contribution to their country that can be recognized for years to come as a major factor in securing our freedom for future generations.

Irreversible Trusts

Charitable fund raisers have been successful when they take the long look. Colleges, universities, and non-profit organizations that solicit gifts do not always receive those gifts at the moment they are promised. Many gifts are given in the form of irreversible trusts.

By law, a person can give a sizable gift of property to his or her favorite charity. Then the person can continue to enjoy the capital earnings of that property or live in that property during his or her lifetime. The children can also be allowed to live in the property after the parents have died, and in some cases, even the children's children can benefit before the property is turned over to the charitable organization.

But in the meantime, the original donor can take the tax deductions of the gift. For example, Mr. and Mrs. Smith live in a home valued at $500,000. They want to live in the house during their lifetime. They also have a child and want the child to live there after they are gone. They turn the title of their house over to their favorite charity, whether it is a church, a university, or a hospital. Based on its current appraisal value, the Smiths claim a sizable tax deduction that reduces their tax payments for the rest of their lives. And yet they and their child can live in the house.

Many systems and procedures in operation today offer great incentives for people to give enormous as well as small gifts to charities. In a similar manner, an enormous amount of private capital in property and various equities could be left in wills and estates to the Federal Debt Reduction Bank of the United States with the understanding that the estate would be used to liquidate the federal debt.

Does this sound far-fetched? Was it crazy for us to think that we could raise $20 million from voluntary gifts to pay for an all-glass cathedral? Yes! But big ideas do come to pass. And when a big idea holds the prospects of laying a firm foundation that can stand for hundreds of years, we have an idea that can capture people's imagination. We sincerely believe that tens of millions of people would be willing to give whatever they can to secure freedom not only for themselves but also for their children, their children's children, and for many future generations.

Every time we consider a new possibility, we give birth to a new set of problems. Every time we set a new goal, we generate new tensions. Every time we make a new commitment, we can expect to produce new conflicts. Every time we make a positive decision, we can expect to be involved in a new set of frustrations.

Possibility thinking challenges us to exceed our limits. This leads us to our tenth possibility.

Possibility Ten: Encourage Superproductivity by a Supernation

Our country has vast, untapped industrial and information-based potential in existing industries and the ability to create new ones. We have no idea how large we can grow in a healthy economy with low interest rates and virtually no inflation! Our tendency is to estimate our future accomplishments by our past achievements and that too frequently limits our thinking.

Over the last two hundred years the average increase in the gross national product of our nation has been 2 percent per year. Many economists say this is the most we can do in the next two hundred years. But is it? History is no proof of what the future can be, nor should it be the guideline.

Let us challenge ourselves to grow at an increased

GNP of 4 percent, 6 percent, or even 10 percent annually. Is it so unthinkable? Many people will object that such growth will bring back inflation and high interest rates. But will it? In the first quarter of 1984 our GNP grew at an annualized rate of nearly 10 percent. In the second quarter the growth was an annualized 7 percent. Economic predictions for the year end called for between 4 to 7 percent growth. Despite many claims to the contrary, inflation has not reared its ugly head, and interest rates are considerably down from their 21 percent high of just a few years ago. Unemployment has come down from double digits to just over 7 percent. Our expanding economy has produced more than six million new jobs in three years. Superpossibility thinkers ask, "Why couldn't we get the unemployment rate closer to zero?"

As our economy expands at possibility-thinking growth rates approaching 10 percent, vast surpluses of capital would be available to pay off our national debt. Super-productivity by a supernation is the most beneficial way to pay down the debt. Everyone will benefit. It is the total fulfillment of the American dream—growth and prosperity for all!

During times of national crisis, such as World War II, our country had a phenomenal growth in GNP. In 1940, there was a 10 percent growth, followed by 25 percent in 1941, 26.7 percent in 1942, and 21.3 percent in 1944.[1] People sacrificed, saved, and cut back to achieve the goal of winning a war. Everyone worked more and spent less. It is possible to become a superproductive nation. Today our national debt constitutes no less a national crisis and deserves our full and utmost commitment. America must learn to be cutthroat in its competitive efforts in the free world market. This means productivity so great that we would be exporting cars to Japan!

We must not look at our reflection in history to set our

limits for the future. Last year in the Rocky Mountains a bighorn ram approached the home of Ed Bailey while he was watching football on television. The bighorn stopped suddenly, seeing its reflection in a plate glass window. Thinking it was another ram, the bighorn bowed its head, ready to charge. He backed up and immediately saw that the other ram backed up too. Every time he moved, his reflection moved. Finally after a three-hour duel, the ram shook its head and charged full force into the window, knocking himself unconscious.

Like the ram in the Rocky Mountains, if we focus on our reflection in history, we will be our own worst enemy. We must not look at the past to measure what we can achieve in the future.

America is a superpower with superpeople who have superpotential for superproductivity. All we need is some superpossibility thinking!

9

A Declaration of Financial Independence

The famous philosopher Sören Kierke-
gaard told the story of a flock of geese
that prepared to fly from the cold re-
gions of Norway to the warmer southern climates in their
annual winter migration. After their first day's journey the
geese settled in a farmer's field where they found a huge
harvest of gathered corn. They quickly gobbled up their
food, curled their necks to tuck their heads under their
wings and, with full and satisfied stomachs, slept until
morning. Awakened with the dawn, the geese stretched
their long necks, looked into the crisp blue sky, and obeyed
their instinct as they flew off to complete their migration.

But one goose could not resist the temptation to remain one more day to indulge in the extravagance of the
food around him. He stayed behind, confident that he could
catch up with the flock the next day. The second day the
goose awoke with an even larger appetite, for his stomach
was stretching from his daily indulgences. The more he ate,
the more he wanted. He was hopelessly and helplessly ad-
dicted to what seemed to be an unending supply of miraculous wealth. Days stretched into weeks as the goose kept
eating his fill of the farmer's food.

One morning, a cold and biting wind awakened the
goose with a start. Rain fell from thick, gray clouds and
quickly turned to ice at his feet. Alarmed by a revived in-

stinct to survive, the goose stretched his neck, spread his wings, and began to waddle, then run as fast as he could. He had to leave today. Tomorrow would be too late. But why couldn't he run faster? Why did his legs move so slowly? Why were his wings so heavy? Why did his heavy body not lift to the wind?

Belatedly, the goose discovered his tragic fate. He had waited too long, indulged too recklessly, ignored the call of his inner instinct too often. Now he suffered from the inevitable consequences of his pitiful procrastination. He could not take off because he was too fat to fly!

How serious is the economic situation facing our country? Have we been overindulging? Are we resisting or ignoring our instinctive call to self-sacrifice, self-denial, and self-discipline? Could we face the same fate as the fatted goose?

What is the greatest problem facing America for the next twenty years? There will probably not be a famine in America in the proportions of the one that haunts Ethiopia. Pockets of hunger? Yes. Famine? Hardly. Not many Americans would predict a nuclear war launched by the Soviet Union against the United States as long as we maintain sensible defensive strength. We may fear the prospect of the thermonuclear war, but such fear is not widely verbalized lest it becomes a self-fulfilling prophecy.

But a vast and growing majority of United States citizens are suddenly becoming painfully aware of an economic crisis that looms over the horizon if we keep traveling the road we are on today!

An economic holocaust is certain if we, like the fat and distracted goose, continue to procrastinate. We are creating a legacy of debt and financial bondage for our children. The following projections of what will happen if we do not reduce the government program deficit are frightening.

- Annual budget deficits will grow from $200 billion in 1985 to $9.5 trillion by the year 2005.

- The debt will escalate to $43.7 trillion by the year 2005.
- The annual interest payment on the nation's debt will equal $9.5 trillion, 34 percent of the entire output of our nation's goods and services.
- The average American citizen's debt of $7,714 will increase to more than $155,000.

Such a situation would be so unstable that before these projections could come true, banks would fail, interest rates would rise beyond what we have experienced, and a worldwide recession would occur. That is why the following questions will not go away.

- If the government has to borrow hundreds of billions of dollars a year simply to pay the interest on the debt, where will the money come from for banks to lend to individuals for the purchase of homes, cars, and refrigerators?
- With the small amount of lendable money left over, isn't is likely that interest rates will soar? After all, the law of supply and demand will not disappear.
- How will our children and grandchildren be able to afford a house? Where will they get the money to make the astronomical monthly mortgage payments?
- How will our country handle massive unemployment when businesses foreclose and factories shut down because they are unable to meet their obligations?
- Will America, limping in financial fatigue, see its influence and benevolent power reduced drastically? Will its power to help oppressed nations overcome their poverty, famine, and disease be virtually eliminated?

• Will an economically crippled United States lose its power to maintain world peace? Will there be aggressive nations that wait like devouring beasts to leap on the wounded, weaker prey in the world?

A Declaration of Financial Independence

The power of being debt free is the power of financial independence. It is the power to promote peace, prosperity, and human pride worldwide. Of all people in history, Americans enjoy more freedom than have any other citizens of any other country ever known. How did we come to this freedom? It happened when people of vision, courage, and integrity signed the Declaration of Independence and then formulated the Constitution with its Bill of Rights. These documents guarantee to every citizen in America the right to pursue peace, happiness, and the the path of prosperity.

You can be a millionaire! You can enjoy the power of becoming a financially independent person if you make a decision to save wisely, invest smartly, and live with long-range goals. For instance you could spend $2,000 this year on a home entertainment center or a trip to the Caribbean. Or you could invest it in an Individual Retirement Account (IRA). To invest it means you must reduce your disposable income this year and give up the home entertainment center or the trip. It means you must exercise some self-sacrifice, self-denial, and self-discipline. But if you invest $2,000 each year in an IRA account that earns 13 percent interest, you will have $182,940 in twenty years, $351,700 in twenty-five years, $662,630 in thirty years, and $1,235,499 in thirty-five years. That $1,235,499 could earn more than $160,000 in interest annually.

The truth is, each of us has the freedom to choose to become financially independent on a personal level. We can enjoy the feeling of being debt free and of knowing that we are giving that sort of heritage to our children. With this freedom comes the feeling of having the power to choose a variety of options in our personal lives.

What is true for individuals is true for our country also. America can know the power of being debt free, but like the individual who invests in an IRA, the American people will have to make a decision to save wisely and live with long-range goals. We will have to exercise some self-sacrifice, self-denial, and self-discipline.

The other key to financial freedom is time. Anyone who sets aside $2,000 a year can become financially independent, but that person must have time to pull it off. A twenty-year-old woman or a thirty-year-old man has the thirty-five years of wage-earning time necessary to build a fortune of $1.25 million. Most fifty year olds do not. The key to financial freedom is to begin *now* and have enough years that will work for you. The longer you wait to begin, the harder it will be.

Today, America's debt, huge though it may be, is still manageable in the sense that if we take action now, we can eliminate the debt and discover the joy of financial freedom. But *we must take action now*. The energy and the enthusiasm that come from anticipating the fulfillment of this dream will release forces for productivity that will generate growth in gross national product. Then that growth will hasten the arrival of the golden future.

Once an individual or institution catches the vision of being forever debt free, the positive motivation and compulsion to thrift catch on. The motivation becomes a movement. With mounting momentum, the movement attracts forces that mysteriously appear to lead the impossible dream to startling, stunning success.

When is success really achieved? At the moment of triumph? At the moment of conquest? No. Success is achieved at the moment of decision. Decisions that become commitments hold within themselves certain seeds of success. Decisions become confident commitments that somehow the wheel will roll; the ship will float; the pistons will fire; the atom will split; human beings will fly faster than the speed of sound; we will walk on the moon!

Today we who live in America enjoy the freedom to make decisions that are commitments. We have the freedom

- to choose our careers,
- to purchase our homes,
- to select the state and community where we wish to live,
- to manage our incomes,
- to launch our own businesses,
- to succeed—and to fail,
- to exercise our faith,
- to plan a family,
- to speak our minds, and
- to practice the religion of our choice.

We are the envy of nations around the world. Of all people on earth, we are most blessed because we enjoy the benefits of a historic decision that was made in 1776. Once in human history a firm decision was made to declare that we would become and forever remain an independent nation. The price paid by our founding fathers who signed the Declaration of Independence has been documented. Their sacrifice was tremendous.

In the past two hundred years enormous prices have been paid to protect, preserve, and pass on that freedom to each one of us. The price can be measured by counting the white crosses in Flanders Field in France, in the Philippines, in the Punchbowl in Hawaii, and in many foreign countries. For two hundred years our best and brightest young men willingly put on the uniform and marched off to defend the inherited freedoms of our land.

Our country was founded on personal sacrifice that arose from a decision that led to a commitment. Each generation for the past two hundred years has had its own unique and timely challenge that if its members had selfishly chosen to ignore or neglect, our freedom would have been lost forever. All that is required for the grand and glorious American experiment to die suddenly is for only one generation to fail in meeting and fulfilling its historic responsibility.

Do we naively think there is no price that *we* have to pay to preserve and perpetuate our inherited freedom to future generations? The unique historical challenge that comes to our generation today is to embark on a war against poverty and oppression. An institution not committed to improving itself is bound to decline. Our challenge is to improve the living standards in America for unborn generations by supplementing the 1776 Declaration of Independence with a 1985 Declaration of Financial Independence.

Attitude and Commitment

We *can* succeed. Our children can know a country that is financially free, but that will require an attitude and a commitment on your part and mine. A positive attitude arising from a firm belief that we can succeed is essential, but action is also necessary. A careful decision that leads to a strong commitment is necessary to accomplish our goal, no matter what the cost. This commitment will forever shape the future destiny of our nation and people. It's not too late. We are young enough as a nation to set a goal today and know we can make it.

Recently a young couple moved from Connecticut, where they lived in a mobile home, to Nashville, Tennessee. There they found a small house, which to their delight they were able to secure with a small down payment and a long-range mortgage. It is a modest home but a beautiful one.

Now they enjoy the pride of ownership! Their comment upon moving into their own home was touching. They said, "We thought we had been born too late!" They had thought they were among the newly married couples of the late twentieth century who, because of high interest rates, could no longer fulfill the American dream of owning a home of their own. Their financial future, they thought, had already been stolen from them by those who had already built up a staggering national debt.

It is not too late if we act *now*. We shall *declare war on the national debt*. In the process, we shall declare war on the poverty certain to fall in catastrophic proportions upon our children if nothing is done today. We shall declare that a fiscal plan will be established to guarantee that our children and grandchildren can own a home of their own in a beautiful new suburb or a comfortable apartment in the city.

But the time is rapidly running out.

Listen! Can't you hear the clock ticking?

Decisions must be made today, or our children will, in fact, be born too late!

Take Action Now!

What can you do now? In a nation of possibility thinkers, you can do many things. Join the growing consensus of concerned Americans committed to paying off the national debt. Either join a movement or start one. The national debt may seem like an incredible mountain to move, but remember, when movements mount, mountains move! We will mention just a few of the things you can do.

1. Get together a group of women committed to paying off the national debt. If you are already involved in a women's group, share with them your concern and the facts given in this book. Get them involved. After all, their children and grandchildren will have to suffer if nothing is done about this national problem.

A group of dedicated women can accomplish amazing victories. In the early 1960s, Brazil was threatened with a Communist revolution. The nation was ruled by morally corrupt men who allowed themselves to be manipulated by Communist subversives. Through a concerted effort on the part of thousands of concerned citizens, the Communist threat in Brazil was finally defeated.

> To the women of Brazil belongs a huge share of the credit for stopping the planned Red takeover. By the thousands, on a scale unmatched in Latin American history, housewives threw themselves into the struggle and, more than any other force, they alerted the country. "Without the women," says one leader of the counterrevolution, "we could never have halted Brazil's plunge toward communism. While many of our men's groups had to work undercover, the women could work in the open—and how they worked!"[1]

If you are not a part of a group, then start one. If there is no leadership, then take on this responsibility. There is a critical need for dynamic leadership. American women need to have the same fervor to battle this threat to our economic freedom as Brazil's women had in battling the Communist threat to Brazil's political freedom. They said,

> This nation which God has given us, immense and marvelous as it is, is in extreme danger. We have allowed men of limitless ambition, without Christian faith or scruples, to bring our people misery, destroying our economy, disturbing our social peace, to create hate and despair. They have infiltrated our nation, our government administration, our armed forces, and even our churches with servants of totalitarianism.[2]

After you read this book, share it with ten other people who can catch the vision!

2. Write your representative and senators about your concern over the rising federal debt and deficits and about

your desire to see the debt paid off. Letting your elected representatives know how you feel is still one of the greatest privileges you have as an American in a democratic system. Your letter will be read, and it will have an influence. Can you imagine the effect you and others would have on the senators and representatives if suddenly forty to fifty million Americans flooded their desks with mail demanding that government waste be controlled, a balanced budget be enforced, and a plan implemented to pay off the national debt?

Let your representative and senators know that you will vote in the next election based on how they handle this important national issue. After all, you want leadership in government that will provide for the future, not borrow from it. If you don't know the name and address of your representative or senators, contact your local library or call the Capitol Building at 202-224-3121.

3. Encourage others to write their representatives and senators too. Your children in grades three through six should write these officials to ask them to please save the future for them. High school and college students (a powerful voting group) could form a lobby and pressure their elected officials in Congress to pass legislation and enforce laws to lead toward a balanced budget and to pay off the national debt. Wouldn't it be wonderful if students across the country on university and college campuses gave as much enthusiasm to this purpose as they did in the past to demonstrations for peace?

4. Lend your support to national organizations committed to balancing the budget. The National Taxpayers Union, 325 Pennsylvania Ave., Washington, D.C. 20002, is a Washington-based lobby that seeks to control government spending and waste of your tax dollars. Its phone number is 202-543-1300. The Foundation for the President's Private Sector Survey on Cost Control, Inc., 1511 K Street, N.W.,

Suite 600, Washington, D.C. 20005, continues the study and monitoring of government expenditures begun by the Grace Commission. Its phone number is 202-628-6428.

5. Contact the producer of a local radio talk show and suggest to him or her that they devote a week to the subject of the national deficit and the debt. They can have as their guests representatives, senators, economists, syndicated news columnists, and chief executive officers of local organizations to discuss their views and concerns.

6. Contact your local newspaper to ask it to have various editorials on the deficit and the debt. You could submit one to be included for publication. Feel free to draw from the material in this book as you write your editorial.

7. Many radio and television stations devote a few minutes each evening to a commentary of interest to their viewers. Ask the station manager to air some commentaries on the national debt issue. Perhaps you yourself could be given time to speak out on this issue.

8. Join *The Committee of Ten Million*. This committee is dedicated to securing by December 1, 1985, ten million signatures of American citizens who want to balance the budget and repay the national debt. If one hundred thousand persons each gathered one hundred signatures, or if one million people each gathered ten signatures, there would be ten million names to give to the president of the United States and to Congress. What a terrific gesture that would be to demonstrate the concern and commitment Americans have toward achieving the goal of financial independence! When you have finished reading this book, collect one hundred or more signatures and mail them to

The Committee of Ten Million
c/o THOMAS NELSON PUBLISHERS
Nelson Place at Elm Hill Pike
P.O. Box 141000
Nashville, Tennessee 37214-1000
Attn: Paul David Dunn, Executive Chairman

Since these petitions will be sent to the president and to Congress, it is important that they be in the correct form. Each petition should be on one side of 8½-by-11-inch paper with the wording of the petition at the top of each page. Each individual must *print* his or her name and address, including zip code, as well as sign the petition. It is also important that each person sign one of these petitions only once.

We will present these petitions to the president as soon as we have ten million signatures or in January 1986, whichever comes first.

PETITION
to the President of the United States
and
to the Congress of the United States

We the undersigned are concerned with the economic crisis that looms because of our current federal budget deficits and increasing national debt. We therefore request that the president of the United States and both houses of Congress work together to balance the budget and take positive steps to repay the national debt.

Signature   *PRINT Name and Address (including zip code)*

_____   _____
_____   _____
_____   _____
_____   _____
_____   _____
_____   _____
_____   _____
_____   _____
_____   _____

9. Contact your representatives in your state legislature and share with them your concern over the national debt crisis. In 1984, more than $90 billion in grants went directly to state and local governments from the federal government. A commitment on the part of state and local officials to the value of paying off the national debt will make it easier for federal officials to balance the budget. Ask your state representatives to keep you informed as to how federal funds allocated to your state are being used. Explain that you will support representatives who responsibly use your tax dollars.

10. In this book, we have listed ten possibility-thinking solutions to the debt crisis, but surely there must be more. Why don't you, the reader, play the possibility thinking game and come up with three, five, or ten new solutions to repay the debt? Send them to us so that we can channel them to the appropriate congressional and senatorial authorities. Send your suggestions to *The Committee of Ten Million* at the address given above.

We have a dream for a debt-free America. Won't you help us make it a reality? Let's believe it can be done. Let's work to make it happen. Let's start today!

The First Step

The spring sunshine cast its warm rays on the young family standing at the entrance to the hospital. The government official had left as quickly as possible after delivering the bill for $7,714. The parents stood stunned in silence. The young father looked at his wife. A tear rolled down her cheek. "It's not fair!" she sobbed. The proud father hugged his wife and child. "No, it's not fair. But it would be more unfair to our child if we did nothing about it. If we start today, we can pay this bill for him so that he can begin his adult life debt free!"

Appendix I

★

ASSUMPTIONS

As we began work on this book, we very quickly realized that different economists and groups used different figures for the same thing. One report would have one figure for the national debt, while another report would have a different figure. The difference, of course, arises from differences of definitions and assumptions when compiling the figures. In addition, change has occurred with increasing speed in recent years. No longer do interest rates, for instance, stay fairly constant for years on end.

As much as possible, we have tried to be consistent in our use of figures throughout this book. When we quote others, however, consistency is impossible. We have used the following figures:

1984 federal debt	$1.836 trillion
1984 federal budget deficit	$164.5 billion
Interest paid in 1984 on the debt	$114.3 billion
1984 population	238 million

The report prepared by Arnold Packer for the Hudson Institute (see Appendix II) contained a number of forecasts, and we tried as much as possible to use those forecasts as normative for consistency's sake. Selected highlights of those forecasts are as follows:

	1984	1990	1995	2000	2005
Gross National Product (in current dollars, trillions)					
Muddling Through	3.683	5.822	8.261	12.196	17.465
Debt Elimination	3.683	6.030	8.767	13.096	19.078
Population (millions)	238.2	252.0	262.2	271.5	280.4
Federal Government Receipts (in current dollars, trillions)					
Muddling Through	.711	1.257	1.823	2.753	4.015
Debt Elimination	.711	1.343	1.986	3.006	4.406
Federal Government Expenditures (in current dollars, trillions)					
Muddling Through	.876	1.460	2.087	2.996	4.245
Debt Elimination	.876	1.384	1.951	2.778	3.958
Federal Government Surplus or Deficit (in current dollars, billions)					
Muddling Through	− 164.5	− 202.8	− 263.9	− 242.3	− 230.1
Debt Elimination	− 164.5	− 41.1	35.4	228.0	447.7
Interest on Federal Debt (in current dollars, billions)					
Muddling Through	114.3	230.5	323.7	439.7	537.1
Debt Elimination	114.3	132.9	110.1	69.5	− 24.1

Appendix II

★

ELIMINATING THE FEDERAL DEBT

A Hudson Institute Paper prepared by Arnold M. Packer under the direction of Jimmy W. Wheeler, Director of Economic Studies.

EXECUTIVE SUMMARY

The study examines the costs, benefits, and plausibility of a fiscal strategy to eliminate the federal debt over an extended period of time. That is, is it wise and possible for the U.S. government, first to eliminate the deficit and then run sufficient budget surpluses to reduce and then eliminate the debt? The answer is "yes" to both questions.

The problem was examined by making twenty-year economic projections for three scenarios:

1. The *debacle* occurs with a simple continuation of the current fiscal stance. That is, expenditures on programs *exclusive* of paying interest on the debt outstrip revenues by $45 billion annually (i.e., the "program deficit" remains at $45 billion). It is extremely implausible that the U.S. political economic system could sustain such a burden: an economic debacle would therefore occur well before the twenty-year period ends. Assuming economic growth at 2.5 percent annually, no recessions, little inflation, and interest rates rising ½ percent annually, the interest on the debt alone would equal 34 percent of GNP by 2005. Even if interest rates remain constant, interest payments would equal one-fourth of GNP by 2015.

2. *Muddling through* is a scenario in which too little action

is taken too late. Even assuming no recessions, no significant interest-rate increases, and no adverse expectations in financial and foreign exchange markets, muddling through requires large program surpluses to pay the growing interest payments on the debt and keep annual deficits in the $200–$300 billion dollar range.

3. *Debt elimination* is a scenario of promptly adopting a long-term fiscal policy of moving toward an annual surplus, and paying off the debt. In addition to the steps required to muddle through, taxes must increase $10 billion more (or spending increase $10 billion less). To offset the effects of a tighter fiscal stance on economic activity, this scenario has the money supply grow 1 to 2 percent more rapidly each year for fifteen to twenty years. This strategy not only avoids the debacle, it substantially improves investment, productivity, and the balance of payments relative to muddling through.

The main cost of eliminating the debt is a higher tax rate (or lower spending) and a corresponding reduction in after-tax disposable income *until* the goal is achieved. The income reduction would be about $150 (in 1972 dollars) per capita. Sometime between 2000 and 2005, however, the tight fiscal policy could be reversed and per capita disposable income would be higher than in muddling through.

In summary, the economic fiscal benefits of moving promptly and decisively to eliminate the debt are great. Neither the required policy steps nor the economic transition are extraordinary, though the political resistance to even smaller changes has proven extremely difficult. However, the dangers of doing nothing are extraordinary. Very good luck on uninterrupted economic growth *and* stable interest rates only postpone the debacle. More likely assumptions, especially with regard to the expectations in financial markets about the reliability of the U.S. government, suggest a crisis before the end of the century.

I. THE BASIC QUESTION: ARE WE HEADING FOR DISASTER?

This report seeks answers to questions about what the U.S. should do about the federal debt and why. These questions need to be viewed from two perspectives: the costs and benefits of a growing debt versus the costs and benefits of its elimination.

A. *Dangers of a Growing Federal Debt*

Will the growing federal deficit—i.e., recurring annual deficits:

1. Inevitably cause a recession or worse?
2. Inevitably lead to inflation?
3. Increase interest rates or keep them high?
4. Keep the dollar overvalued and increase our balance of payments deficit, or bring the value of the dollar down so quickly on foreign exchange markets as to disrupt the economy?
5. Seriously impair government operations and the ability to meet its obligations (e.g., defense and social security)?
6. Ultimately lower the U.S. standard of living?
7. Reduce the funds available for investment in other countries and thereby harm the international economy, particularly the developing countries?

Since the answers to these questions range from maybe to almost certainly, these same questions, asked from the other side of the coin, probe the costs and benefits of eliminating the debt. There is no question that in principle the federal debt can be substantially reduced, perhaps even eliminated, by running substantial surpluses over time. The issues facing the U.S. government are how can this be done, technically and politically. Indeed, even more important than determining how to reduce the debt is first making the judgment whether it is really worth doing. Without a consensus on this point, debt reduction will not occur. Determination of whether there are substantial long-term gains to debt reduction is the main purpose of this paper, especially as regards the implications for employment, inflation, interest rates, the balance of payments, the U.S. government, and the world economy.

B. *Approach and Basic Assumptions*

It is fashionable when answering questions about the debt to compare alternative economic scenarios. I will follow fashion and use three scenarios: debacle, muddling through, and debt-elimination. The differences among the alternative scenarios will depend on a number of factors. Some of the factors will be evaluated and others will be assumed to be either unimportant or unmeasurable.

I will assume that expectations that the deficit will increase inflation or lead to a recession have no effect on economic behavior, *except* when the debacle hits. I will also assume that monetary policy is used to offset the effects of changes in the budget, and aims for and hits a target for the growth in nominal GNP. Moreover, I will assume that the nominal GNP target is identical for all three scenarios. This implies that a larger deficit does *not* cause a larger growth in the money supply, which has been the more common post-World War II experience. On the contrary, the opposite occurs; the larger deficit implies a slower growth in the money supply to offset the fiscal stimulus caused by the deficit (the more recent experience of 1980–84).

The assumptions are clearly unrealistic in the "long run". Depending on the fiscal/monetary strategy chosen, expectations, politics, and policy will change. The government cannot allow interest on the federal debt to take a larger and larger share of GNP. Ultimately, the resultant political pain will force action, which may have to be taken in a crisis atmosphere. Similarly, interest rates may become unacceptably high with the monetary authorities then moving to accommodate the debt, fueling inflationary expectations. Obviously, these and other assumptions are possible.

The assumptions used in this paper are conservative with regard to the conclusions reached. That is, alternative assumptions make the dangers of continued deficits, or the benefits of reducing the debt, even greater than concluded here. More realistic assumptions would only strengthen the paper's conclusions that the best strategy the country could follow is to move quickly and strenuously to reduce or eliminate the debt.*

The choice among the three scenarios is a policy choice among three economic strategies which ultimately will have major macroeconomic (i.e., recession, inflation, and interest rate) implications. For example, in the debacle scenario, when foreign and domestic lenders begin to doubt the U.S. government's ability to redeem its debts—without debasing the currency—interest rates will increase and a serious recession will ensue. When confidence in the U.S. government's ability to repay its debt—and, therefore, confidence in the U.S. dollar—is shaken, the value of the dollar will also fall rapidly. A rapidly falling dollar will be inflationary, as the prices of imports and import-competing goods thus rise sharply and are felt throughout the economy. Since interest rates rise substantially in this scenario, and take off dramatically when confidence collapses, a likely Federal Reserve policy response would be to increase the money supply very rapidly, with strong inflationary repercussions. This response would invalidate the previously mentioned assumption about the monetary policy offsetting fiscal stimulus.

In addition to these macro implications, there are important long-term structural implications of choosing among the sce-

---

*At various points in the text the effects of particularly binding assumptions will be noted.

narios. The choice will affect investment, exports, productivity, industrial composition, and financial portfolios. Again using the debacle scenario as an example, productivity and investment will fall with large long-term losses in economic growth and living standards. Wealth held in financial form will be seriously reduced and many financial institutions will fail.

Thus, each of the three scenarios has a macro story and a structural tale. In this paper, the short run will be identified with the macroeconomic implications; it ends when the economic transition—caused by the chosen fiscal policy—begins. This is an unconventional use of the term short run, which serves mainly to identify a point of transition. For the debacle and muddling through, the short run will end when expectations about a crisis mount. The time-to-crisis cannot be predicted. *For purposes of the numerical analysis, I will assume that the short run extends through the year 2005. In reality, the short run will be shorter than that; it will end when expectations change reality.* For the debacle, the short run may be five to ten years. For muddling through, the short run will clearly end before the century does, because expectations will make the outcome nastier than the simulation exercise presented below suggests. For eliminating the debt, the transition is defined in terms of the effects on disposable income of the population.

The scenarios are:

(1) *The Debacle*: Deficits grow exponentially as interest payments on the growing federal debt increase. The debacle occurs when bondholders lose confidence in the dollar and U.S. capacity to meet its obligations. In this scenario, the short run is before the loss in confidence and the long run begins when the debacle occurs.

(2) *Muddling through*: Sufficient action is taken to keep deficits in the $200-$300 billion range but not to balance the budget or reduce interest rates. In this case, the short run is until the structural effects of the debt begin to affect the U.S. standard of living adversely in a perceptible way.

(3) *Eliminate the Debt*: Sufficient action is taken, first, to balance the budget, and then to run a surplus. As a result, interest rates decline, the debt is reduced and, after a long period, eliminated or brought down to some target level (such as equal to some measure of public investment). In this scenario, the short run is

the transition period during which disposable income is reduced to move from a deficit to surplus position and, ultimately, to debt elimination. The long run is after disposable income exceeds that of the previous alternative.

The key short and long run characteristics of the scenarios are:

SCENARIO	SHORT RUN	LONG RUN
1. Debacle	Exponentially growing debt and rising interest rates.	Crisis of confidence in the dollar and U.S. debt.
2. Muddling Through	Debt grows at $200 to $300 billion annually and constant interest rates.	Risks of later debacle rise; structural changes in the economy are perceptible, especially slow productivity growth and declining manufacturing sector.
3. Eliminate Debt	Taxes increase and/or spending decreases and lower interest rates.	Per capita disposable income higher than alternatives, more robust manufacturing sector.

C. *Summary of Results*

The table at the end of this section briefly summarizes the situation at the assumed point of transition, i.e., twenty years from now in the year 2005. Clearly, the debacle scenario cannot reach that far: spending 56 percent of the GNP for interest on the federal debt (or borrowing that amount politically) is virtually impossible. The debacle's real proximity depends on what happens to real interest rates. More accurately, the ratio of real interest rates to the growth of real GNP is what really matters. Since I assume that real GNP growth is approximately the same under all three scenarios, real interest rates are the crucial variable.*

Assuming a continuation of current budget trends and even if real rates stay constant (at 8 percent) while the deficits increase, the interest on the debt will reach an unsustainable 14 percent of GNP in the year 2005. It is much more likely that real interest rates will rise, as the government demand for funds continues to rise. If the rise is modest (about 25 basis points annually), interest payments on the debt will be 30 percent of GNP in 2005 and would equal the GNP in 2115, except that the debacle would surely come earlier. If real interest rates rose 50 basis points annually, then interest payments on the debt would reach more than half of GNP in 2005 and would equal GNP in 2008. As soon as 1995, the interest payment would consume an unsustainable 13 percent of GNP.

---

*This assumption presumes that the monetary-fiscal policy-mix differences between the scenarios can be implemented. In reality the politics of the time almost certainly would result in different growth rates. In most cases, the probable differences intensify the conclusions reached in this paper.

Muddling through requires belated fiscal discipline to eliminate the program deficit and then, as years pass, partially offset the growing interest payment on the still-growing debt. This strategy, of doing too little too late, permits the debt to climb to $5.9 trillion, which is slightly smaller relative to GNP than the current debt, assuming no increase in interest rates. Interest on the federal debt would be 3 percent of GNP, about two-thirds of what will be spent for social security. Although this does not appear particularly onerous on the surface, the government has to run surpluses except for interest payments, and the private sector is facing permanent high interest rates. Clearly, the muddling-through scenario would be more difficult if expectations worsened in a way that increased interest rates (for example a weakening of the confidence of foreign investors in U.S. government obligations, with a resulting capital outflow), and/or a recession, intervened.* In that case, investment and productivity would be less, the debt would be higher and the situation would resemble the debacle scenario.

An effort to eliminate the debt could be successful before 2005, based on the policy changes that are not so large as to be economically unrealistic. Although the recent past has shown that even smaller budget changes have led to virtual gridlock in Congress and between Congress and the White House, the required changes also are not so extreme as to preclude a bipartisan compromise. In light of the positions taken by both sides in the 1984 election, such a compromise would require public retraction on important statements by the president and committed leadership in both parties, especially the Democrats. Whatever the details of the compromise, the longer term payoff is high. Taxes would have to be increased and/or spending reduced. Tax increases are used in the example, but the situation is exactly the same if the spending cuts are in entitlement or other transfer programs. (Analytically, these are negative taxes.)

In addition to what is needed to muddle through, the tax-rate increases required to eliminate the debt are not especially large; 5 percent for individuals and 15 percent for corporations were the values used in this estimate. Moreover, the increases are phased in gradually over twenty years. The money supply has to grow 1 or 2 percent more rapidly each year to offset the effects of fiscal restraint on economic growth. The economic results provided by the simulation are reasonable: real interest rates stay

---

*A major risk to this scenario would be one of attempting to inflate out of the constraints on current spending in the face of adverse economic conditions.

positive and reflect real investment opportunities, and none of the other variables move beyond past experience.

As the debt is reduced, real per capita income, investment, productivity, and exports are higher. Moreover, since taxes could be *reduced* to eliminate the no-longer-necessary surplus before 2005, disposable per capita income would even be higher at the end of twenty years, if a debt-elimination strategy were chosen and successfully followed, than if the country chose to muddle through. However, until the goal is achieved and taxes reduced, debt elimination would require a temporary reduction in disposable income. The reduction would be about $150 to $175 (in 1972 dollars) per capita per annum relative to muddling through. Two-thirds of the reduction would come from the tax increase and a third from reduced interest income (because interest rates decline).

The conclusion is that the benefits of reducing or eliminating the debt are great. The dangers of doing nothing are monumental, even if—as this study shows—recessions, inflation, and other unpleasant surprises are never encountered. Unfortunately, the public has become immune to the cry of danger, because the short run dangers of deficits have been overblown. At any point in time deficits need not cause inflation or recession and, if private demand is weak, deficits need not raise interest rates unduly. However, continuous large deficits and an exponentially growing debt add up to an unsustainable long run strategy. The 2005 projections are summarized below:

SITUATION IN YEAR 2005

Scenario	Debt $Trillion	Deficit $Billion	Debt/GNP %	Interest/GNP	
				% in 2005	% in 2008
1. Debacle*	43.7	9545	257	56	96
2. Muddling Through	5.9	230	33	3	
3. Eliminate	0	0	0		

*Assuming a 50 basis point increase in real (and nominal) interest rates annually.

II. SHORT RUN IMPLICATIONS

The seven questions listed on the first page of this paper have different answers in the short and long run. The macro implications—recession/inflation, interest rates, and the dollar/balance-of-payments—change between short and long run. The structural implications—the government's capacity to meet its obligations and the impact on the standard of living here and abroad—occur slowly and are not very evident in the short run.

A. *Implications for Recession and Inflation*

In the short run, there is no reason to believe that recession is more likely with a growing deficit than with a declining one. Practically, it may be easier to operate the economy with an expansive fiscal policy (growing debt) and tight money (high interest rates) than otherwise. Monetary policy is easy to change. If interest rates are high and inflation is low, the Fed can lower interest rates quickly when demand falters. Lower interest rates will quickly lead to increased spending for housing, autos, etc. Thus, over the next few years, there is no reason to believe that the deficit will cause a recession. This conclusion is consistent with most economic forecasts; few are predicting more than a temporary slowdown in economic growth.

Nor, given the assumptions, is inflation more likely with a big deficit in the short run. Instead, there is reason to think the opposite. A deficit—that is, fiscal stimulus—will produce monetary restraint, i.e., tight money.* Both dominant schools of economic thought believe that tight money will reduce inflation. Depending on their prejudice and training, economists either argue that an excess supply of money causes inflation (if the economist studied at Chicago) or that excess wage demands are the culprit (if he/she studied at MIT or Harvard). The lower money supply will be less inflationary if Chicago is right and a overvalued dollar will do the same trick for the Keynesians. Tight money increases interest rates which increase the value of the dollar which keeps the smokestack industries (e.g., steel) uncompetitive in world markets. With unemployment relatively high and profits relatively low, the unionized smokestack workers are modest in their wage demands. The non-inflationary behavior of these pattern-setting unions would, according to Keynesian economists, set a moderate and non-inflationary pattern for the economy.

---

*Of course, a major political change could lead to an attempt to finance the deficits with expansive monetary policy. The result would be inflation followed by recession as expansive policy would be replaced by severe tightness to bring inflation back under control. The paper's assumption is based on the judgment that, having paid this price already, the U.S. is unlikely to shift to inflationary policies.

B. *Interest Rates*

Almost all schools of economics argue that interest rates will be higher with a larger deficit. The Reagan Administration disagrees, but even that disagreement disappears if the following assumptions are accepted. Presumably, there is some increase in interest rates that will offset the macroeconomic impact of an increased deficit. As stated previously, I assume that such an offset is achieved by the Federal Reserve. That is, the Fed targets nominal GNP growth rates and adopts a monetary policy to hit that target; the result of these *assumptions* is that employment and inflation are approximately the same regardless of the deficit. The larger deficit will, however, require (or cause) correspondingly higher interest rates to achieve this offset. Thus, real interest rates have been at historically high levels in recent years.

According to the Wharton model, used in this study, a deficit difference of $470 billion (in 2000) is offset by about a 550-basis-point increase in long-term interest rates (nominal).* That is, offsetting the fiscal stimulus of a $470 billion deficit requires that the Fed let interest rates be 5.5 percent higher than they would otherwise be. Indeed as shown below, the nominal interest rates assumed in the debacle scenario are not excessive in light of the expected deficits. Compared to "muddling through," interest rates before the debacle are "only" 320 basis points higher in 1995 and 630 basis points higher in 2000. With the deficit approaching *$1 trillion* by 1995 and ($3 trillion by 2000) in the debacle, these interest rate assumptions could be low. The debacle interest rate could easily exceed 20 percent by the year 1995, triggering a crisis by then.

Assuming, very conservatively, that the short run lasts for at least twenty years, to 2005, the nominal interest rates in the three scenarios are shown below:

	1984	1990	1995	2000	2005
Moody's Corp. Bond Rate					
Debacle	13.7	15.5	18.0	20.5	23.0
Muddling Through	13.7	13.8	14.8	14.2	12.4
Debt Reduction	13.7	8.6	8.6	8.7	7.6

---

*The Wharton annual econometric model is used to estimate the various economic changes that occur with the policy shift required to move the U.S. from "muddling through" to "debt elimination." Although differing in detail, any of the major models would produce similar results for the variables of interest to this analysis.

C. *The Value of the Dollar and Balance of Payments*

The usual story is that higher interest rates will enhance the dollar and lead to an increase in its value. The more highly valued dollar—because it makes U.S. goods relatively expensive—will increase U.S. imports and discourage exports. The overvalued U.S. dollar is now blamed for most, if not all, of this nation's balance-of-payments deficit, which will exceed $100 billion on the merchandise account this year. A 300 basis point fall in interest rates will decrease the dollar's value by some 15 percent, changing exports and imports by 6 to 8 percent each. According to the Wharton simulations, the net exports of the U.S. will be more than twice as high if the debt-reduction scenario is followed than if this country muddles through. In the debacle scenario the dollar stays very high until the crisis, when it plummets.

III. LONG RUN STRUCTURAL CHANGES

A. *Impact on Government's Ability to Meet Its Obligations*

Now, we begin to get to the heart of the problem. First, let me define the "program deficit" as the difference between revenues and all expenditures *except* interest on the deficit. *The situation is unstable if the current program deficit of $45 billion is maintained* "as far as the eye can see" and then some. Yet, the Congressional Budget Office (CBO) estimates a $45 billion program deficit for the rest of the decade.

With inflation at 5 percent, revenues over the next six years have been estimated (by the CBO) to increase a little more than 10 percent annually (in nominal dollars). Without major policy changes, spending will increase almost as fast. With inflation at 5 percent, national defense expenditures will increase more than 10 percent a year. The number of social security recipients will grow 2.7 percent annually (compared to only 1 percent in the last six years). Real per person benefits for Medicaid are estimated to grow 4.3 percent annually. Moreover, 85 percent of transfer payments are estimated to grow 9 percent annually through the end of the decade.

These factors imply little, if any, reduction in the program deficit, *unless* painful actions are taken to reduce spending or increase taxes. Interest rates will stay high and interest payments on the growing debt, and the debt itself, will grow exponentially.

The government will be less and less able to meet its obligations for defense, social security, or interest on the debt. With this fiscal posture, a debacle will occur.

Even if sufficient action is taken to keep overall deficits in the $200 to $300 billion range and "muddle through," the growing interest payments on the growing debt continue to eat away at the government's capacity to perform. To muddle through, the government will have to take in $310 million more than it spends on programs in 2005 to cover part of the interest payments on $540 billion; yet, there will still be a $230 billion deficit. In this case, however, real default is averted.

By 2005, if the debt were eliminated, the federal government could spend all its income on programs. Achieving the goal, however, would require discipline over the next fifteen to twenty years. In the year 2000, for example, while muddling through would require a $200 billion program surplus, the debt-elimination strategy would require a $300 billion program surplus. That is, until the goal is achieved, costs would be incurred. But, much would be achieved. Debt elimination, by getting the government's house in order, allows the U.S. to control its fiscal destiny instead of being at its mercy. A comparison of the three situations is shown for 2000 and 2005.

FISCAL SITUATION IN 2000 AND 2005

Scenario	(Deficit) or Surplus	Interest on Debt	Program (Deficit) or Surplus
		($ Billions)	
2000			
Debacle	(3160)	3115	(45)
Muddling	(240)	440	200
Debt Elim.	230	70	300
2005			
Debacle	(9545)	9500	(45)
Muddling	(230)	540	310
Debt Elim.	-0-	-0-	-0-

B. *Impact on the Standard of Living*

In the short run, the standard of living of the average American does not vary a great deal under the three scenarios. In the short run, GNP grows in the range of 2.5 percent annually in each of the scenarios (a little faster if the debt is being reduced and interest rates are lower, and a little slower for the debacle). Because population growth is only half as great as GNP growth, per capita income will increase.

In contrast, per capita disposable income is highest in the debacle scenario because taxes need not be raised nor government expenditures reduced to control the deficit. In effect, today's standard of living is increased to the detriment of the future. Disposable income is lowest under debt elimination, because the country is in the process of getting back on a "pay as you go" basis.

The positions of these two polar scenarios are reversed after the debacle when confidence in the ability of the government to repay its obligations begins to erode seriously. Then, the ensuing recession reduces the average standard of living substantially.

Muddling through occupies a middling position in both the short and long run. Higher interest rates and more current consumption imply less investment and slower growth in U.S. productive potential than if a debt-elimination strategy were followed. Although the growth rate potential is only likely to be a fraction of a percent lower than under the debt-elimination strategy, the accumulated annual differences add up as the time horizon lengthens. By 2005, overall productivity is 2.2 percent greater if debt reduction, rather than muddling through, is the chosen strategy. Moreover, investment in fixed non-residential investment is 15 percent higher.

Thus, in the short run and the long run, per capita income grows most rapidly under the debt-elimination scenario and most slowly under the debacle scenario. However, the growth in *disposable* income is the reverse in the short run because of the higher taxes and/or lower spending required to correct the fiscal imbalance. Yet, the fiscal position must ultimately be reversed in any scenario. For example, after the debacle, something will have to be done to pay off a portion of the debt, which will be astronomical by then. Moreover, because of the lower investment coupled with the recession, the tax-rate increase will have to be much larger than if action were taken now.

The same considerations apply, although with less force, when comparing the debt-elimination to muddling-through scenarios. A bigger tax increase or spending reduction will be required to fix the situation in twenty years than if it were done now, because the deficit will be four to five times larger by then. Moreover, it will be less affordable because the economy's potential will be growing more slowly. In contrast, it will be possible to reduce taxes in 2005—because the debt will be eliminated—if action is taken now. Thus, in the long run, both per capita income and per capita disposable income grow faster under the debt-elimination scenario than if the U.S. muddles through.

The following caveat must be kept in mind in evaluating the previous statement. The improvement in living standards under the debt-elimination scenario will come about only if monetary policy indeed keeps the economy on a constant track. There was more investment in 1984 with a large deficit and no recession than there would have been with a smaller deficit and a recession. In other words, *the benefits of debt elimination are only realized if the Fed offsets the fiscal restraint with monetary ease*, and keeps the economy on a steady growth path.

C. *Impact on Living Standards in Other Countries*

In 1984, U.S. investment will total about $400 billion. The deficit in the current account will exceed $100 billion, equal to about one-fourth of investment in plant and equipment. Part of investment (and some part of U.S. consumption as well) is financed by overseas savings. Does this mean less investment is going on abroad? Maybe, and maybe not. Many Third World countries facing serious debt service constraints at present need to be reducing their debt, not increasing it. Selling more to the U.S. than they buy here is a way to do that. Nor is Europe straining its productive capacity when unemployment rates are in double digits in many European countries. The fact that many U.S. companies are now borrowing, long-term, in European markets, however, can only be discouraging investment there.

It is unlikely that U.S. foreign borrowing is reducing anyone else's investment by anywhere near the $100+ billion U.S. current account deficit. Higher than necessary U.S. interest rates are, however, drawing funds from other countries and discouraging some investment there. In some countries, the investment discouraged (by higher interest payments) will be greater than that encouraged (by the export sales generated by the overvalued dollar). In other countries, the reverse will be true and there will be a net increase in investment. Surely, the net is negative in high-debt countries whose debt-service burdens are sensitive to international interest rates.

In the long term, even under the muddling-through scenario, the living standards of the rest of the world can only suffer if the U.S. soaks up a substantial portion of the world's savings to finance consumption here. The real fall in the world's living standard, however, will occur with the debacle. The financial disruption and the U.S. recession will shrink markets and decrease employment worldwide.*

---

*The world is entering a phase of massive labor force growth. Although the labor force in the industrial world has almost stopped growing, that in the develop-

IV. THE DEBACLE: CORRECTION THROUGH CRISIS

A. *Scenario Characteristics*

Rates of growth, inflation, and interest shape the scenario. Most important is the ratio of real interest rates to the real rate of GNP growth. In some sense, the situation is not unlike that of corporation investment. If a firm borrows at an interest rate that exceeds the rate of return, then eventually it will go bankrupt. Interest payments take a larger and larger share of corporate income. Borrowing for current consumption or eating the seed corn is not a viable long-term strategy for individuals, corporations, or governments. The nation's economy cannot possibly sustain another twenty years of the current fiscal strategy of spending $45 billion more each year on programs, net of interest, than it collects in revenues.

B. *Changes in the Financial and Economic Structure by 2005*

Continuing on the current fiscal path will rapidly change the nation's—and the world's—financial structure. By 2005, if the federal government is to succeed in unloading an additional $43.7 trillion in debt obligations, the public will have to be holding thirty-three times as much federal debt as it does now.

It is not helpful to think of the bond-holding public as little old ladies in tennis shoes or coupon-clipping tycoons. Most of the holders of the obligations will be pension funds, banks, money market funds, corporations, and other institutions. Some of these large institutions will be American and some will be foreign (including foreign governments). While statistically it may make a difference whether the payments are made to American or foreign institutions, the practical difference is likely to be small. Citibank and Exxon will shift out of dollars into yen or marks as quickly as Credit Suisse or Royal Dutch Petroleum. Nor will the former's interest income be much more likely than the latter's to end up as salary checks for average U.S. workers.

---

ing world is now increasing in response to the reductions in infant mortality that took place there a generation ago. The world needs to generate *one billion jobs in the next quarter century* to keep unemployment and underemployment from growing even more than it is now. And "now" includes double digit unemployment rates in Europe and widespread un- and underemployment—and its attendant poverty—throughout much of the developing world. Reducing the waste of irreplaceable human resources is surely among the criteria against which any U.S. budget policy should ultimately be measured.

Asking the U.S. and foreign "public" to hold an additional $40 trillion in U.S. government liabilities will require higher interest rates. The bondholders will also reduce their holdings of other liabilities. Some of those unfunded liabilities represent loans that would have been made to finance productive plants and equipment. Thus, somebody's standard of living will be lower as a result of the deficit.

This is another way of saying that the U.S. government deficit consumes a large fraction of the world's saving that would otherwise finance investment. The U.S. deficit is the mechanism that permits Americans to consume today at the expense of tomorrow's production. In the year 2000 of the debacle scenario, the deficit will be almost three times greater than corporate profits, instead of two-thirds as great, as it is in 1984.

C. *The Long Run Crises*

A debacle is unavoidable if the current fiscal policy of spending $45 billion more for programs (net of interest on the debt) is continued for very long. Even if interest rates do not rise, inflation is only 5 percent, and the business cycle is tamed while deficits run trillions of dollars annually, a crisis is not avoided. The debacle scenario is based on the conservative assumption that, until the crisis occurs, real GNP grows by 2.5 percent annually—despite these incredible deficits.

A more reasonable assumption is that the enormous deficits will increase interest rates, even if they do not affect inflation or unemployment. If the interest rate rises ½ percent annually, then in about twenty years (2005), the debt will be about 2.5 times the GNP and interest payments will equal 56 percent of GNP. If such an arrangement could last for twenty-five years—which it assuredly could not—then, in 2010, the interest on the debt of $130 trillion would be 129 percent of GNP.

These extrapolations are clearly unrealistic. The current total federal budget now represents about one-fourth of the GNP. Sometime well before interest on the debt reaches 25 percent of GNP, investors will make similar extrapolations. Investors will then decide that the risk of repudiation of the debt or intentional inflation (to reduce the ratio of interest payments to GNP) is too great. They will sell U.S. government obligations to reduce their risk and find that there are no buyers—domestic or foreign. Prices of government securities will fall; that is, interest rates will rise. Then the country will be in a financial and economic crisis, i.e., the "debacle" will occur.

Banks will fail and credit will be abruptly restricted. The linkages among nations are now so numerous that the repercussions will not be restricted to the United States: the result of the debacle will be a severe worldwide recession.

V. MUDDLING THROUGH: THE PATH TO STRUCTURAL DETERIORATION

A. *Scenario Characteristics*

Since the dire implications of the debacle make it an unlikely outcome, muddling through is much more probable. In this scenario, the government is responsible enough to eliminate the program deficit with one sort of "down payment" or another. But the Administration and Congress together do not have the political will to eliminate the deficit, let alone run a debt-reducing surplus.

In the muddling-through scenario, deficits remain in the $200 to $300 billion range, a diminishing share of the growing GNP. The ratio of debt to GNP falls modestly. Even this is the result of some painful fiscal policy.

The important implication—of both the debacle and muddling through scenarios—is the growing difficulty of correcting the situation. The longer corrective action is postponed, the larger and more painful that correction must be. Of course, the difficulty grows more quickly in the debacle, but it also occurs, in a different way, in muddling through.

B. *Structural Changes by 2005*

The muddling-through scenario also changes the structure of the U.S. economy in an adverse way. Real interest rates remain in the 8 to 9 percent range until close to the very end of the twenty-year period; as a result, the value of the dollar remains relatively high. The overvalued dollar continues to erode U.S. international competitiveness. Relatively high interest rates, coupled with the loss of opportunities in international markets, discourage business investment. High interest rates also reduce personal investment in housing and interest-sensitive durable purchases such as autos. Thus, investment, exports, and durable manufacturing are not as strong as they might be if the debt were reduced.

Financial portfolios become more weighted with government obligations as they increase and private financial placements decrease. By assumption, unemployment and inflation remain under control, but investment and productivity are arrested relative to the debt-reduction scenario. If expectations really count, then investment and productivity will fare less well than assumed in the scenarios and reported below.

C. *The Long Run Malaise*

This scenario is more likely to end with a whimper than a bang. By 2005, productivity increases are only slightly more than 1 percent annually, about the same as increases in per capita disposable income. Fixed investment is growing slightly faster than assumed in the scenario and GNP.

The biggest problem will be government finances. In 1971, the debt service was 1.4 percent of GNP. By 2005, the federal debt is close to $6 trillion and interest on the debt is 3 percent of GNP. As a result, by 2005, the *program surplus* must exceed $300 billion to keep the *federal deficit* at $230 billion. Of course, the biggest risk is that the fiscal discipline needed to obtain that program surplus may be no more evident in 2005 that it is today. The result then will be something more like the debacle than muddling through. If the country began a program *now* to arrive at a program surplus *smaller* than that required under muddling through in 2005, then the debt could be eliminated by 2005. Taking such action now, rather than postponing it to future administrations, is a very difficult leadership issue, in light of the 1984 campaign promises and the policy differences between the parties. The payoff is high and the opportunity provided by 1985 is greater than is likely to be the case until perhaps 1989.

This is the most important lesson of the exercise. If a program of fiscal discipline were started now—that was not much more painful than what will have to be done anyway by the year 2000 to avoid a debacle—the nation would be measurably better off in the beginning of the next century.

VI. ELIMINATING THE FEDERAL DEBT: A COMMITMENT FOR THE FUTURE

A. *The Debt-Reduction Scenario*

The primary fiscal policy assumptions in the debacle scenario are a budget policy that maintains the current $45 billion deficit in the program budget, and a monetary policy that offsets this stimulus and maintains economic growth at 2.5 percent annual rate forever. The primary economic assumptions are a growing real interest rate (the product of monetary policy offsetting the growing fiscal stimulus) and a stable inflation rate. The interest/ GNP ratio grows quickly, because the real interest rate exceeds the economic growth rate by a substantial margin.

Muddling through moderates the deficit and real interest rate problems but does not eliminate them. The program deficit is eliminated by 1988, and a program surplus exceeding $300 billion is achieved by 2005, just to offset interest payments and keep total federal deficits in the $200 to $300 billion range. Real interest rates are relatively constant. Yet, deficits continue, the debt continues to grow, and the real interest rate continues to be more than double the real growth rate.

The alternative described in this section contains a very different budget policy assumption, namely, that the current $45 billion program deficit is eliminated completely by 1986 and the overall federal deficit is eliminated by 1991. Moreover, the budget surplus exceeds $200 billion by the year 2000. The fiscal restraint reduces real interest rates to approximately the rate of economic growth. The budget surplus would exceed $400 billion by 2005. Taxes can then be reduced, because the entire debt will have been eliminated.

The crucial policy assumption is that monetary policy will respond strongly and promptly to the fiscal discipline. If monetary policy keeps interest rates high, neither the budgetary nor economic benefits will ensue. Indeed, much if not all of the budget savings accomplished during 1982–84 was offset by increased interest payments on the debt resulting from higher interest rates. More importantly, if interest rates do not decline, the fiscal restraint will reduce economic growth during the period. Recessions will occur, producing larger deficits and less investment—just the opposite of the results sought.

In order to maintain a 2.5 percent rate of economic growth, the assumption is that there will be 14 percent more money (M2) by 1990 and 16 percent more by 1995 and beyond under this scenario than under muddling through. That is, M2 grows about 9 percent annually over the next decade rather than about 8 percent if the nation muddles through. The offset does not require an extraordinary monetary policy, on the contrary, only 1 or 2 percent faster annual growth than projected under the standard Wharton long-term projections.

The economic assumption is that the reduction in federal borrowing—coupled with the faster growth in the money supply— lowers the real interest rate by two percentage points (200 basis points) on average in the first five years, another 200 basis points in the next five-year period, and finally levels off in the waning years of the century. That is, the nominal corporate interest rate is about 8 percent and the real rate is 3 percent, which is about five percentage points less than the rate under muddling through.

The lower interest rate causes real investment, productivity, exports, and economic growth to accelerate. By the end of the twenty-year period, the increases in the levels of these four crucial variables—relative to muddling through—are: investment 13 percent, productivity 2.2 percent, exports 6 percent, and economic output 3 percent. These differences are important enough to change the structure of the U.S. economy, as discussed below.

B. *Structural Changes by the Year 2005*

Because economic growth exceeds the real interest rate, the federal government's interest burden declines. Once the program surplus exceeds the interest payment on the federal debt (in 1991), the government actually runs a surplus and the federal debt begins to diminish. The reduction, slow at first, accelerates. In 2000, the debt is only 12 percent of GNP; it is totally eliminated in 2004. As emphasized many times before, the Federal Reserve is assumed to offset the fiscal changes, keeping the economy more or less on track.

Compared to muddling through, the U.S. economy in the year 2005 is quite different if action is taken now to reduce or eliminate the debt. Consumption is 1 percent lower. Export and capital industries are larger, while the service industry is slightly smaller than it would be under the muddling-through strategy.

The financial structure of the country and the world is also quite different under this scenario. Not only is there more liquidity, there are almost $6 trillion less U.S. government liabilities. Presumably, investors and financial institutions will be holding commercial paper and corporate bonds instead. Compared to muddling through, the value of the dollar will be about 20 percent less. The U.S. will be a capital exporter and foreign debtors will have a much reduced debt burden for themselves—and ourselves—to worry about.

While this altered economic and financial structure will have obvious benefits, the policy also has its costs: higher taxes and/or lower federal spending. (If the expenditure reductions are in entitlements or other transfer payments, then these are reductions in so-called negative taxes, tantamount to a tax increase analytically. Tax increases were used in the simulations for computational and semantic ease.) Before examining the costs and benefits of such a debt-elimination strategy more systematically, a case needs to be made for the plausibility of the political assumptions.

C. *A Debt-Reduction Strategy—"Fail-Safe" Budgeting*

Deficits have always been with us, so why should anyone expect things to change? Those who have worked with federal budgets know about the "bow wave" effect. The deficit almost always looks smaller three years off than it does when the three years have passed. An unexpected recession has intervened. Or errors in estimates of spending and revenues were resolved in ways that increased the deficit. There is a serious discipline problem because resisting program or tax changes that "only" cost a few billion dollars is not worth much political capital compared to either a $200 billion deficit or a budget re-estimate that exceeds the painfully achieved savings. Therefore, a billion dollars is lost in this tax loophole and that expenditure program; as a result, the deficit keeps growing.

This same "bow wave" effect is noted by winning presidential candidates. The candidate blames his predecessor for being unable to balance the budget and pledges that—if elected—he will achieve that goal by the end of his term. Four years pass and, unfortunately, the deficit gets bigger.

What causes the continued and growing deficits? Is the culprit economics, politics, procedures, or all of the above? Deficits are often needed to achieve important national goals—e.g., to fight a war or to offset the effects of a recession caused by a rise in energy prices or one caused by tight money. But deficits also arise because politicians do not have the courage to bring spending and taxes into balance.

Procedural problems also increase deficits. Mistaken predictions of future economic performance, interest rates, or other "exogenous" factors and surprises often confound the President's Office of Management and Budget, the Congressional Budget Office, and others that make budget estimates. The erroneous forecasts almost always lead to an increase in the deficit, not an offsetting reduction in spending elsewhere or an offsetting tax increase.

The proposed balanced budget amendment (like the Budget Act of a decade ago) is an attempt to establish a new procedure that would contain the damage of political and forecasting failures. The proposal had legislative and economic flaws. A workable alternative would recognize that deficits are sometimes needed to offset a lack of demand but recognize that this tactic is no excuse for not reducing the debt over the business cycle. The alternative would have to set out a debt-reduction goal that would have a good chance of being achieved. More important than the particular goal is the mechanism for achieving it. It is crucial that the mechanism be believable—otherwise the necessary monetary policy and interest rate offsets may not be forthcoming. A possibility is to make achieving the debt-reduction goal "fail-safe." One possible mechanism is described below.

For example, if the prescribed path for deficit reduction was not being followed, then prespecified taxes would increase or preselected expenditures would decrease *automatically*, unless Congress overrode the automatic controls. In the case of an "override," the Congress would have to put forth an alternative plan for reducing the debt over the business cycle. Of course, the deficit or debt goal would be over the business cycle, so that fiscal policy would remain as a viable economic policy tool.

In such a mechanism it may also be necessary to preselect the fiscal policy changes to be used countercyclically. Preselection would increase the probability that the changes are indeed temporary and do not offset the long run plan to reduce the federal debt. That is, a positive or negative tax surcharge or a temporary job program would be the predetermined countercyclical tool. The preselection—like the automatic stabilizers in the budget—will also tend to reduce the policy lag that often makes anti-recession corrections too big as well as too late.

Any such mechanism would be a major legislative change. Obviously, making such dramatic changes in executive branch and congressional treatment of tax and spending decisions is not an easy political task. It will first be necessary to convince the public that the benefits of reducing or eliminating the federal debt far outweigh the costs. Making such a case is the central purpose of this paper. The precise details of the political compromises required to implement the policy change can only occur in the give and take of the political process; as noted above, only general characteristics can be discussed here.

VII. COSTS AND BENEFITS OF ELIMINATING THE DEBT

A. *Costs of Alternative Goals*

The benefits of reducing or eliminating the debt are great. The fact that it is not being done is proof that the costs must also be formidable. The debt-reduction scenario described in the previous section raised corporate and personal income taxes by $5 billion annually from 1985 to 2005. Thus, corporate and personal income taxes will each be $100 billion higher in twenty years than they would be if the country muddles through.

These revenue increases require an effective personal tax rate about 5 percent higher (by 2004) than current law permits.

The effective income tax rate would be 14.25 percent on an average, rather than 13.5 percent. The effective corporate tax rate would be 15 percent greater or 27.5 percent in 2004 rather than 24 percent under muddling through. Despite the higher corporate tax rates investment is greater because the lower interest rates more than offset the higher taxes.

These tax increases can be reversed once the chosen debt-elimination goal is achieved. Until then, unless expectations make muddling through worse than assumed, the higher personal income tax rates will not be fully offset by greater economic output. Thus, although real per capita GNP is 3 percent greater under the debt-elimination scenario, per capita disposable income is 2 percent less in 2004 and almost 3 percent less in 1997. (The tax increase is not the only income reducing feature of eliminating the debt; lower interest rates also reduce the income of savers.) However, the reduction in disposable income is temporary and could be offset before 2005 by tax reductions as the debt is eliminated. The "cost" of debt elimination—that is, the number of years the higher taxes and lower disposable income must be endured—depends on how the "debt elimination" is defined.

At least four possibilities present themselves. One is to eliminate the entire debt, including the debt held by the trust funds. (Trust funds—such as those backing the social security system—hold government debt in their portfolios. At present, somewhat over $400 billion of federal debt is in trust funds.) A second possibility is to eliminate only the debt held by the public. The goal could be to bring the debt to some arbitrarily selected fraction of GNP (e.g., 25 percent). The goal could relate the debt to the federal "capital budget."

Adopting the last goal would make the government more "businesslike" in its budget policy. Businesses are not debt free buy try to use short-term loans for working capital and long-term loans for income-producing assets such as capital investment. The capital-budget concept may be difficult to implement because of definitional difficulties, e.g., defense weapon systems have long lives but do not produce income. Do they belong in the capital budget? How about education?

According to the simulation, the total debt would be eliminated in 2004. In that event, a balanced budget, instead of the $447 billion surplus implied by the assumed policies, will be the fiscal target in 2005, the final year of the simulated period. Therefore, a substantial tax reduction could be made in 2005. If the goal is to eliminate only the debt held by the public, then the tax reduction could come a year earlier and eliminate the surplus of $382 billion projected for 2004. If the capital assets of the government were estimated (arbitrarily) at $800 billion at the end of the century—and reducing the level to that target is the goal—then the tax reduction could arrive in 2001 to wipe out that surplus of $207 billion projected for that year.

Whichever goal is chosen, small tax reductions would probably start a few years earlier than the end of the period. This would eliminate the shock to the economic system of a very large increase in disposable income, the oversized surpluses, and stretch out the time required to achieve the goal. The bottom line is that the tax decrease would reverse the results for per capita disposable income after the goal is achieved. Instead of being about $150 (in 1972 dollars) lower, per capita income would be about $150 *higher* (again in 1972 dollars) in 2005 if prompt action is taken to eliminate the debt rather than the more likely event of muddling through.

In summary, compared to muddling through, *the certain costs of the debt-elimination strategy are higher taxes (or lower spending) and up to a 3 percent (or about $150 to $175 of 1972 dollars) reduction in per capita disposable income for a period of fifteen to twenty years.* About one-third of that is lower interest income—because interest rates are lower—and the rest is the result of higher taxes (offset, in part, by faster economic growth). For many, however, the only certainty about the future is death and taxes. Hastening either is generally unattractive.

B. *The Benefits*

The most important benefit of following the debt-elimination strategy is preventing the debacle. Ultimately, the muddling-through scenario will require the same or greater program surpluses as the debt-elimination scenario. While a truly imminent crisis tends to bring politicians to more courageous action, it may be that the debacle will come too quickly to be avoided. That eventuality is more probable if a recession begins in the next few years, once again swelling the deficit as it did in the first years of this decade.

Moreover, even compared to muddling through, debt elimination has great advantages. The nation's economic structure will be more productive. Investment, productivity, exports, economic output, and the housing stock will be higher. Small businesses and state and local government will have less difficulty borrowing and the debt-ridden Third World will have an easier time paying off their loans.

The nation's financial structure will also be more sound. Portfolios will contain private, instead of federal, debt. Monetary policy will not have to bear the entire burden of controlling inflation. Potential conflicts between the domestic goal of price stability and international goals regarding the value of the dollar and related complications can be more easily avoided.

That is, the fear of increasing the value of the dollar may now brake the Fed's willingness to reduce money growth for domestic reasons. Reducing and eliminating the debt will lessen that fear. The concern that the Fed requires federal debt in order to engage in open market operations to control the money supply is misplaced. The central bank can just as easily buy and sell commercial paper and other instruments.

In sum, the economic benefits of reducing or eliminating the debt are great. The dangers of doing nothing are monumental. The challenge is for political leadership to undertake the needed steps. This may require a concentrated effort to convince the public, Congress, and the White House that the costs of debt reduction are worth it benefits.

★ ──────────────────────────────

NOTES

Chapter One

1. The figure of $7,714 was computed by dividing the 1984 federal debt of $1.836 trillion by the 1984 United States population of 238 million.
2. Milton and Rose Friedman, *Tyranny of the Status Quo* (New York: Harcourt, 1983–84), 35.
3. J. Peter Grace, *War on Waste* (New York: Macmillan, 1984), v–ix.
4. See the Hudson Institute Report in this book, Appendix II.
5. Robert M. Dunn, Jr., "Deficit: Interest Threatens to Outpace Growth," *Los Angeles Times,* September 2, 1984, sec. 1, 7.
6. From an interview with John Templeton, who cites "The Historical Statistics of the United States, Colonial Times to 1970" (Washington, D.C.: U.S. Dept. of Commerce, 1976).
7. "Reducing the Deficit: Spending and Revenue Options" (Washington, D.C.: U.S. Printing Office, 1984), 1–5.
8. Grace, *War,* v.
9. Ibid., v.
10. Ibid., v.
11. George Herbert Mead, *Mind, Self, and Society,* vol. 1 (Chicago: Univ. of Chicago Press, 1934), 11.

Chapter Two

1. We must be realistic here because this points up the true danger of debt. Investors who borrow money to buy gold at $35 an ounce and then sell it at $800 an ounce have made a nice investment. Many investors, however, borrowed money to buy gold when it was $800 an ounce, based on expectations that its price would go even higher. When the price declined to $400 an ounce, and lower, instead, they were left not only with gold that was worth only half what they paid for it but also with interest and principal to pay on the debt as well.

2. For a more thorough treatment of the destructive force of a large national debt, see *Debt Shock: The Full Story of the World Credit Crisis* by Darrell Delamaide (Garden City, N.Y.: Doubleday, 1984).

3. Ibid., 157.

4. "The Economic and Budget Outlook: An Update," (Washington, D.C.: Congressional Budget Office, August, 1984).

5. "Baseline Budget Projection for Fiscal Years 1985–1989," (Washington, D.C.: Congressional Budget Office, 1984), 106.

Chapter Three

1. Friedman, *Tyranny,* 12.

2. John F. Kennedy, Inaugural Address, January 20, 1961.

3. "Porkway to Deficit," *Wall Street Journal,* September 7, 1984, 24.

4. Summarized in *Business Week,* June 18, 1984, 15.

5. "Messiah of the Market," *Time,* August 27, 1984, 43.

Chapter Five

1. "Manville's Big Concern As It Files in Chapter 11 Is Litigation, Not Debt," *Wall Street Journal,* August 27, 1982, 1, 8.

2. Barry Newman, "Banker's Delight," *Wall Street Journal,* September 20, 1984, 1, 22.

3. Susan Trausch, "Tackling U.S. Debt, One Drop at a Time," *Boston Globe,* August 10, 1984.

Chapter Six

1. J. Peter Grace, *Burning Money* (New York: Macmillan, 1984), 3.

2. Ibid., 88–89.

Chapter Seven

1. Here is how but one proposed amendment to the constitution reads. This amendment has been awaiting action from Congress since July of 1982!

Article

Section 1. Prior to each fiscal year, the Congress shall adopt a statement of receipts and outlays for that year in which total outlays are not greater than total receipts. The Congress may amend such statement provided revised outlays are not greater than revised receipts. Whenever three-fifths of the whole number of both Houses shall deem it necessary, Congress in such statement may provide for a specific excess of outlays over receipts by a vote directed solely to that subject. The Congress and the President shall, pursuant to legislation or through exercise of their powers under the first and second articles, ensure that actual outlays do not exceed the outlays set forth in such statement.

Section 2. Total receipts for any fiscal year set forth in the statement adopted pursuant to this article shall not increase by a rate greater than the rate of increase in national income in the year or years ending not less than six months nor more than twelve months before such fiscal year, unless a majority of the whole number of both Houses of Congress shall have passed a bill directed solely to approving specific additional receipts and such bill has become law.

Section 3. The Congress may waive the provisions of this article for any fiscal year in which a declaration of war is in effect.

Section 4. Total receipts shall include all receipts of the United States except those derived from borrowing and total outlays shall include all outlays of the United States except those for repayment of debt principal.

Section 5. The Congress shall enforce and implement this article by appropriate legislation.

Section 6. On and after the date this article takes effect, the amount of Federal public debt limit as of such date shall become permanent and there shall be no increase in such amount unless three-fifths of the whole number of both Houses of Congress shall have passed a bill approving such increase and such bill has become law.

Section 7. This article shall take effect for the second fiscal year beginning after its ratification.

2. Lewis K. Uhler, "The Need for a Freeze on Government Spending," *Wall Street Journal,* January 5, 1983, 20.
3. Friedman, *Tyranny,* 65.

Chapter Eight
1. The Council of Economic Advisers' "Economic Report to the President," February, 1984 (Washington, D.C.: U.S. Government Printing Office, 1984), 220–223.

Chapter Nine
1. Clarence W. Hall, "The Country That Saved Itself," *Reader's Digest,* November, 1964, 143.
2. Ibid., 147.

126414